CHILDREN'S SAVING

CHILDREN'S SAVING:
A STUDY IN THE DEVELOPMENT
OF ECONOMIC BEHAVIOUR

Edmund J. S. Sonuga-Barke

Department of Psychology, University of Southampton, UK

Paul Webley

Department of Psychology, University of Exeter, UK

LEA LAWRENCE ERLBAUM ASSOCIATES, PUBLISHERS LEA
Hove (UK)   Hillsdale (USA)

Lawrence Erlbaum Associates Ltd., Publishers
27 Palmeira Mansions
Church Road
Hove
East Sussex, BN3 2FA
UK

British Library Cataloguing in Publication Data
Sonuga-Barke, Edmund J.S.
   Children's Saving: Study in the Development of Economic Behaviour.–
   (Essays in Developmental Psychology Series, ISSN 0959–3977)
   I. Title   II. Webley, Paul   III. Series
   155.4

   ISBN 0-86377-233-1

Cover by Joyce Chester
Typeset by DP Photosetting, Aylesbury, Bucks.
Printed and bound in the United Kingdom by Redwood Press Ltd.,
Melksham, Wiltshire

For Funké and Julie

Contents

Acknowledgements   **xi**

1   A new focus for the study of children's economic affairs   1
Introduction   1
The standard cognitive developmental approach   2
The socio-developmental approach   5
The types of economic problems to be solved   6
The complementary nature of formal and functional aspects of children's
    economic affairs   7

2   Children's saving as an example of economic development   9
Introduction   9
What is saving?   10
Current theories about why people save   10
Saving from the socio-developmental viewpoint   12
Children's saving: the existing literature   13
Outline of the studies to follow   15

3   The development of functional saving in a play economy   17
The development of saving as a response to income constraint   17
Study 1: Choices under income constraint   19
Results   23
Discussion   25
Study 2: Saving—a response to different types of threats   27
Results   29
Discussion   32

Study 3: Choosing between actions with social or economic value   33
Results   37
Discussion   40
The development of saving revisited   40

4 **Extending the boundaries of the play economy   43**
Introduction   43
The status of the board game play economy   43
Institutionalised saving   44
The relationship between the development of saving
    and consumer strategies   45
Study 4: Money management in a more naturalistic setting   45
Results   50
The changing understandings of saving; form and function   51
Discussion of Study 4   59

5 **Social influences on children's saving   63**
Introduction   63
The development of economic ideals within popular culture   63
Representations of economic actions; some general considerations   64
The historical context   65
The marketeers' view of saving   66
Study 5: Encouraging adult saving   67
Results   67
Comment   68
Study 6: Encouraging children's saving   69
Results   70
Comment   71
Parents' influence on children's saving   73
Study 7: Parents' views of children's saving   73
Results   74
Parents' views of children's economic competence: saving as an antidote to
    economic madness   81
Comment   83

6 **Contrasting the economic, social, and developmental significance of
    young children's behaviour   85**

7 **First commentary: Cognitive approaches to economic development revisited,
    by Anna Emilia Berti   91**
Introduction   91
The "standard cognitive-developmental approach"   91
The socio-developmental approach   93
Board game play economies   95
Saving in a play economy and in real life   97
The developmental trends and their explanations   99
Children's conceptions of banking   100
Conclusion   103

8   Second commentary: How and why children save, by Sharone L. Maital &
    Shlomo Maital   105
    Introduction   105
    The theory of economic socialisation among children; towards an eclectic
      ethological approach   106
    The ecological model   108
    Do results on children's saving cross cultural borders?   114
    Willingness to defer gratification and subjective interest rates: psychological
      foundations of children's saving   116
    Saving: A response to income constraints or a product of them?   118
    Economic socialisation: thoughts on intervention   121
    Conclusion   122

9   An epilogue: towards an integral developmental economic psychology.
    A reply by the authors   125
    Introduction   125
    Concerning the metatheoretical principles of an integral developmental
      economic psychology   127
    In summary   137

References   139
Author Index   149
Subject Index   151

Acknowledgements

Many people have contributed in one way or another to the research described in this book. But three people have been especially important; Stephen Lea, Mark Levine and Alan Lewis. Each has played an important role. Stephen Lea introduced us both to economic psychology and jointly supervised the PhD research on which Chapter 3 is based. His clarity of thought and lucid writing style have helped us immensely. Mark Levine collected much of the data presented in Chapter 4 and the second part of Chapter 5. Luckily he did not just do as he was told but improved on rather sketchy plans and later provided excellent draft reports. It was also a pleasure to play football with him. Alan Lewis collaborated on the research reported in Chapters 4 and 5 and we have benefited both intellectually and socially from working with him. Without his drive half of the research reported here would not have been carried out at all and this book benefits greatly from his contribution.

Other people have helped in a variety of ways. Rachel Kirby sorted out our often convoluted computer programs; David Taylor built beautifully finished mock shops and banks; and the secretarial staff of the psychology department, particularly Joan Fitzhenry and Angela Boobyer, dealt with phone calls from parents, and our demands, with unfailing patience and courtesy. The graduate students of the department contributed statistical advice and lots of moral support. Most of all we must thank the children and parents who took part and the innumerable headteachers and staff who let us circulate leaflets and appeal for volunteers.

Financial support for the research was provided by the Economic and Social Research Council in the form of a studentship to Edmund Sonuga-Barke, the Halifax Building Society, who gave two grants with no strings attached, and the University of Exeter, who provided both grant and travel money. We are especially grateful to Caroline Smith of the Halifax Building Society for her help and her cogent comments on the research. She kept us in touch with the commercial side of children's saving.

Part of the book was written while Paul Webley was on sabbatical leave at Erasmus University Rotterdam. We are grateful for their hospitality and financial support.

1

A New Focus for the Study of Children's Economic Affairs

INTRODUCTION

The workaday world of economics is, as sin was to Chesterton, practical as potatoes. To talk of economic endeavour is to talk of the application of practical means to material ends. The means may be complex and relatively removed from the face to face interaction of the market place, particularly in technologically advanced societies, but they nevertheless embody the practical goal of personal well-being or the well-being of others. As the economics textbooks would have it, economics is essentially about the distribution and allocation of scarce resources. Paradoxically, although essentially practical, "the economic" is completely cultural. The value (and therefore the practicality) of economic actions rests on a culturally derived set of ideas both about the legitimacy of certain ends (economic ideals) and the acceptability of certain means. The acceptance of economic endeavour as valued and meaningful rests on culturally derived assumptions about the nature of social reali and the basis of social relations. The practical and cultural significance of "the economic" are intimately intertwined.

Unfortunately, many contemporary developmental psychologists have failed to appreciate either the essentially practical or entirely cultural significance of "the economic" in children's lives. Inspired more by a desire to test the scope of application of neo-Piagetian grand theories of cognitive development than by the challenge of constructing a developmental economic psychology, they have robbed children's economic thought and action of this cultural meaning and as

1

a consequence stripped childhood economics of its practical nature and functional significance.

These accounts have tended to view the emergence of particular ways of thinking about both the social and material world as "natural", "inevitable" and so unproblematic. Not surprisingly they have shown little interest in the process by which certain ways of thinking achieve legitimacy in Western societies (Buck-Morse, 1975). An increasing number of developmental psychologists discontented with the ahistorical nature of these types of accounts of development (Goodnow, 1990; Rogoff, 1990; Light & Perret-Clermont, 1989; Wertch & Younis, 1987) have argued that an analysis of the culture and history of ideas in Western societies is a prerequisite for any study of the social development of children in those societies.

In line with this principle the present book presents an approach that returns practical significance to children's economic behaviour by emphasising its cultural origins. Our goal is to produce an approach that does justice to both the cultural basis and the practical expression of economic thought during development: To provide, in short, an adequate basis for the study of children's economic behaviour. Because of this joint requirement we will develop an approach that addresses the peculiarly practical issues surrounding the development of economic behaviour—an integral developmental economic psychology.

For want of a name we will draw the set of assumptions underlying this approach together and dignify them with the title of socio-developmentalism. Given our emphasis on the practical and instrumental nature of economic thought and action, as well as its cultural origins, our approach could just as well be called socio-functionalism. But whatever the title, the most important point is that the assumptions about the nature of economic activity and human development that form the basis of this approach differ from those implicit within the neo-Piagetian approaches favoured by many scholars in the past.

In the first two chapters we will set the ground work for the empirical studies that follow. In this chapter we will draw out the different assumptions that underpin the socio-developmental approach and compare it with the cognitive developmental approach. By doing this we will try to refocus the agenda for developmental psychologists interested in the economic affairs of the child. We will then go on to relate this new agenda to the study of children's saving.

THE STANDARD COGNITIVE DEVELOPMENTAL APPROACH

Economic socialisation has been the focus of increased interest in recent years. Most research in this field to date has been firmly based within the neo-Piagetian tradition (see Furnham, 1986; Stacey, 1982; or Berti & Bombi, 1988, for reviews of the literature). At its worst (in some of the consumer psychology literature) this has involved a rather mindless search for stages in children's thinking about the economic world equivalent to those found for the child's understanding of the physical world; at its best, it has involved a careful consideration of what factors are responsible for change in these ideas (e.g. Ng, 1983). The research into children's understandings of bank profit is a good example of this.

This has been investigated by Jahoda (1981; 1984), Jahoda and Woerdenbagch (1982), and Ng (1983; 1985). The child's understanding of bank profit develops in fairly similar ways in Scotland, Holland and Hong Kong, although Ng reports two extra stages to Jahoda. In Jahoda's study the children had to imagine that a person deposits £100 in a bank and takes it out after a year. They were then asked whether this person would get back more, the same, or less than was deposited. A similar question was asked about a loan, and the children had to explain their answers as well as estimating the amounts involved. From their answers six levels of understanding were identified. At the lowest level, there was no knowledge of interest at all (about a third of 12 year olds were at this level). At the next, children believed that you get back more money from deposited money but pay back the same on a loan. Clearly, the idea that banks require interest on loans is a difficult concept to grasp. At the next level children realised that interest is payable on both deposits and loans but deposit interest is thought to be higher than loan interest. During the next stage they are seen as equivalent. Finally (a stage reached by only very few 12 year olds and only a quarter of 16 year olds) it is understood that loan interest must be greater than deposit interest. As one child put it (p. 77):

A person puts money in and the bank loans that money out; and when the person gets that money back, there is interest on it. If someone gets a loan they have to pay interest, which is higher than the interest the bank pays you.

Both Jahoda and Ng tried to investigate the processes that are involved in initiating changes in economic thinking by inducing cognitive conflict and contrasts. Conflict between different aspects of a child's understanding or between understanding and observations should result in equilibration. Jahoda asked children to explain how banks got money to pay interest and/or its staff. For all children, but those with a complete understanding, this creates a problem; if deposit interest is equivalent to loan interest how can a bank make any money? In some cases this conflict did result in a development of understanding, as in this case (p. 81):

I: How does a bank get its money? C: (*Ruminates for a while and then says*) The bank has to make a profit somehow, but I've no idea how. I: What does one have to pay back after borrowing? C: (*Triumphant exclamation*) That's how the bank makes its profits.

As well as creating conflict in a way similar to Jahoda, Ng created contrasts by posing parallel questions about saving and borrowing. He found that while conflict did enhance understanding, contrasts had no effect. This kind of research is clearly a fairly straightforward extension of the cognitive developmental approach into the social/economic domain. Indeed, Jahoda (1984) makes it very clear that he is primarily interested in the nature and development of social thinking. As far as it goes, this type of work paints a very consistent picture of the development of children's economic thinking. A number of general trends have been identified. First, there is a shift from confusing natural and social phenomena to differentiating them, and a corresponding shift in differentiating the economic from the social. Second, there is a move from seeing economic norms as "natural" to seeing them as mere conventions. And third, there is a shift from an individualistic perspective to a societal one. This consistency has encouraged a great number of studies, with most researchers around the world reporting similar findings.

This type of research, although interesting and provocative, leaves us with only a partial understanding of economic development during childhood. Its failings are not specifically methodological or theoretical, but rather are to do with the metatheoretical context, the whole cognitive developmentalist agenda, which in many ways follows on from a neglect of the meaning of "the economic" in Western societies.

There are a number of specific characteristics of study set by this agenda that limit its scope. First, a failure to examine the cultural meaning of the economic has led to a nominal definition of economic behaviour. In other words, the form of an action rather than its function defines something as "economic"; buying, saving, borrowing, working etc., are all economic behaviours whereas playing football, talking to friends etc. are not. But aspects of these latter behaviours can be economic (and would be treated as such within a social exchange theory framework) when they involve a behavioural expression of the intention to maximise reward. Second, and related to the first point, economics is seen as something "out" in the adult world that children have to come to understand before they can operate as effective economic agents. So researchers interested in children's economic development have studied the way in which children acquire and reproduce knowledge relating to concepts such as money, the bank, debt, inequality, class, "means of production" and occupation: concepts that allow the growing child to effectively interact with the agents and institutions that constitute the economic sphere of the child's social world (e.g. Baxter, 1976; Berti & Bombi, 1981; Berti, Bombi & Lis, 1982; Connell, 1977; Leahy, 1981; Miller & Horn, 1955; Ng, 1983). They have not examined the economic world that children construct for themselves (Webley & Webley, 1990). Third, and most obviously, the development of economic cognition and the acquisition of economic knowledge has been studied, rather than the development of economic behaviour (Jahoda, 1984). Fourth, they have taken a very individualistic view of the causes of development. Children are supposed to construct their understanding of the complexity of economic relations through individual interaction with the world and this process occurs in an orderly and stage-like way. Finally, this emphasis on the individual has played down the importance of variations in thought that may be due to differences in their content. Signel (1966) demonstrated many years ago that experiential and didactic learning produced different structures. The economic world is probably learned about in both these ways.

THE SOCIO-DEVELOPMENTAL APPROACH

We have a rather different approach. From the viewpoint adopted in this book, the study of the child's understanding of the workings of the adult economy must be placed in its proper context. We see banking, buying, borrowing, and betting simply as formal expressions of the system of values that underlie culture- (or subculture-) specific economic ideals, and as such we see them as representing more or less approved means of fulfilling those ideals.

The developments that lead to economic competence, as defined within a particular culture, involve not just the acquisition of knowledge that allows the child to undertake these operations. It also involves the transmission of an economic identity based on the assimilation of information, originating from a wide variety of sources, about the acceptable goals of practical action or, in other words, the intentions that should govern economic practice. In short, knowledge of that which constitutes economic competence in Western societies is gained so that widespread beliefs about the acceptability of economic goals, or social representations of economic actions (Moscovici, 1984), come to control the actions of younger members of a society. Briefly, our argument is that economic intentions are constructed within the social group and are fulfilled by the practical actions of individuals aided by the availability of formal institutions or economic facilities.

Adopting this view has a number of implications. It becomes important to study the available social representations of economic intentions, their cultural precedent and historical origins. In Chapter 5 the nature of the social representations of acceptable goals of economic action in general, and saving, in particular, held and propagated within English society will be studied. By looking at the way two groups with somewhat different interests in children's saving (those marketing the services of the savings institutions and the children's parents themselves) try to encourage saving in youngsters, we will try to examine the social climate in which children's saving occurs.

The socio-developmental approach also encourages us to adopt a child-centred view of economic activity. Because cognitive developmentalists have adopted a nominal definition of economic activity, there has been little attempt to study children as economic agents in their own right, solving economic problems and constructing their own economic world with such activities as swapping, bartering, betting, and giving presents to friends. The main practical implication of the socio-developmental view is that it encourages us to centre on the child's own understanding of their economic world and the problems presented in it. This involves the recognition that the status of the individual as an economic actor, at least in Western industrialised societies, is defined in terms of their response to problems of resource allocation, rather than just in terms of their knowledge about the working of the formal world of grown-up economic systems, although this knowledge may well help solve these problems.

The child becomes cast as an economic problem solver and economic development becomes defined in broader terms, as the functions of economic activity are emphasised along with their form. There is a shift in emphasis from the formal to the functional aspects of economic activity. While, on the one hand, economic activities can be regarded as expressing a set of culture-bound economic ideals, perhaps based around the intention to maximise individual wellbeing, they can also be regarded as providing solutions to the problems of allocation that are encountered as an individual tries to fulfil these goals. This approach allows a much wider definition of economic activity. It recognises the possibility that although the strategies found within the formal world of adult economics provide effective means of solving these sorts of economic problems, these formal institutions do not need to exist in order for economic action to occur. This has important implications for the study of economic development. This is because before children understand how banks or shops work, what profit is and why daddy goes to the bookmakers every Saturday morning (and why mummy shouts at him when he gets back) they are presented with a continuous stream of problems of resource allocation that, according to the position adopted here, should be described as economic.

THE TYPES OF ECONOMIC PROBLEMS TO BE SOLVED

The socio-developmental view sees the child as an economic problem solver. But what are the features of economic problems? Essentially, these problems are created when children are faced with a situation where fulfilling an economic goal is restricted by limitations on choices (Staddon, 1980); the nature of these limitations being defined by constraints on the allocation of finance, time or energy between a potentially unlimited number of alternatives in the pursuit of individual wellbeing (Ferguson & Gould, 1975).

These constraints, in fact, constitute the primary defining feature of all choice. If you are faced with a choice between visiting the cinema or watching television you can do one or the other but you cannot do both at the same time. In this situation the two activities can be seen as being related by the constraint of having just one choice. The cost of losing the opportunity to go to the cinema provides an objective measure of the value of the chosen activity, watching the television.

But choices are rarely discrete in this way. Individual choices are often limited by more "global" constraints. For instance, most of us only have a limited amount of money to spend, and all have only a limited amount of time to spend doing those things we can afford. When this is the case individual choices become related over time. Choices made in the present are related to choices in the future by the specific nature of the global constraints in operation (Rachlin, Kagel, & Battalio, 1980). The cost of one alternative is not simply the loss of the alternative activity available at a specific time. It is also the loss of opportunity to make certain other choices in the future. The nature of this intertemporal relationship varies according to the type of constraint under which a person is acting.

The ability to adapt to these types of constraints can be seen as one behavioural manifestation of the intention to maximise reward that represents, for many, the legitimate end of economic activity in Western societies (Schwartz, 1975; Sharpe, 1981).

THE COMPLEMENTARY NATURE OF FORMAL AND FUNCTIONAL ASPECTS OF CHILDREN'S ECONOMIC AFFAIRS

Before moving on to apply this analysis to children's saving it is important to stress one thing. While it is clear that the cognitive developmentalist and the socio-developmental approaches make wholly different assumptions about the nature of the "economic" and its meaning in the lives of children, the focus of, and the data originating from those studies inspired by the two approaches are complementary. Insights derived from the present approach give us a new perspective on the findings from previous studies. For instance, studies carried out by cognitive developmentalists have on the whole been concerned with children's thought and action as they develop a "mature" and realistic understanding of their relationships with the agents and institutions that exist within the economic world. The socio-developmental approach places these formal gains in children's economic knowledge in a cultural and functional perspective. This is because from the socio-developmental point of view, coming to know the economic world of institutions serves only to provide one set of solutions to the problems of resource allocation presented in particular cultures with particular histories and particular ideals of practical action.

While cognitive developmental studies have given us an insight into children's understanding of the formal institutions in their economic world, the socio-developmental approach places that world in its historical and cultural context. Whereas the cognitive developmentalists have dealt with the development of relations between the child and other economic agents and economic institutions, the socio-developmental approach deals with the social construction of the economic aims to which those relationships are addressed. In other words from the socio-developmental point of view the social reproduction of knowledge of the practical relationships between agents and institutions subserves the reproduction of social and cultural norms about the practical aims of everyday economic life.

In this way economic development occurs on two levels. One level involves children developing an understanding of the meaning of and requirements for adaptive performance in a particular culture, one expression of which, in Western societies, is the ability to maximise wellbeing by adapting to economic constraints. On the other level, children develop their understanding of practical strategies that allow the effective development of these forms of adaptive behaviour.

2

Children's Saving as an Example of Economic Development

INTRODUCTION

The few psychological studies of children's saving that have been carried out in the past have invariably only touched on the topic indirectly. Children's saving has been seen as a rather minor part of how children learn to buy (Ward, Wackman, & Wartella, 1977) or work (Goldstein & Oldham, 1979) or behave with money (Furnham & Thomas, 1984; Marshall & Magruder, 1960). Saving may have been seen as a factor in a child's economic socialisation (as by Marshall & Magruder) or as a useful childhood predictor of adult economic behaviour (as by Newson & Newson, 1976), but it has not seemed significant enough to deserve full-scale investigation. So why a book on children's saving?

We believe that the development of children's saving offers a particularly clear example of the way the formal and the functional, the individual and socio-historical characteristics of action interact during the child's socialisation to economic competence. Thus saving provides the ideal focus for our new approach to understanding children's economic affairs, in which a child's developing economic thought and action are seen as functional expressions of culturally determined economic ideals put into operation using both informal and formal means.

On a practical level this study of saving allows us to examine how children of different ages solve practical economic problems of workaday life. How do they integrate regular and irregular sources of income to provide for their desired expenditure. How do they learn to protect their savings (and so their future well-

9

being), from optimism concerning their prospects, their impulses, their poor memory and their enemies.

WHAT IS SAVING?

On the face of it this seems a rather unnecessary question. Surely we all know what saving is: it is putting "left over" pennies in a piggy bank or a jam-jar on the mantelpiece; it is putting money into a post-office or bank account; it is investing in pension funds. But it is not as simple as that. Formally, since income must be either spent or saved, saving can be defined as unspent income. If a girl gets 60p pocket money a week and accumulates it for a month to buy a toy for £2.40, she has done a lot of saving per week but none at all for the month. We would presumably want to say that she had saved for the toy. If, on the other hand, she kept her pocket money each week from Saturday until Friday and then spent it all on her youth club subscription would we say that she had saved up until Saturday? Definitions of saving are essentially arbitrary and rely on the specification of a time period.

The economic psychologist Katona (1975) has clarified the issue by making some useful distinctions. First, there is a distinction between voluntary and involuntary saving. Involuntary saving occurs when there is no decision to save. For adults, this might be because they have life insurance, which unknown to them has a saving as well as an insurance component. For children involuntary saving may take place when parents give them money with the proviso that it is saved, perhaps by being put in a post office account. Another distinction is between contractual and discretionary saving. The latter involves a decision to save during a particular time period whereas contractual saving is the result of a decision taken earlier, for example an agreement to participate in a school savings scheme. Although the end result may be the same, that is, a lump sum available for spending, there are important psychological differences between these types of saving. A decision to join a saving scheme, for instance, may be part of a strategy to protect oneself against lack of self-control. Involuntary saving, on the other hand, may be part of a parental strategy to encourage the "habit" of saving.

CURRENT THEORIES ABOUT WHY PEOPLE SAVE

Before we look at the development of saving we need to examine the existing theories of adult saving. Economic theories of saving often have a distinctly psychological feel to them. Keynes (1936), for instance, recognised the importance of individual motives in determining levels of saving and made a series of intuitive guesses about the nature of these motives. His list included pure miserliness, the acquisition of profit through interest, independence, precaution and foresight.

Functional and Non-functional Approaches to Saving

There are essentially two types of theories of saving. These can be distinguished in terms of the importance they place on the economic functions of saving. A number of theories are based on individualistic notions of rational action; these assert that saving is motivated by specifically economic concerns—people save for future consumption or they save for interest. On the other hand there are those that are based on the idea that saving is a socially acceptable goal in itself or the response to a drive developed during early childhood. These theories argue that saving is not motivated by specifically economic concerns. One set of theorists see the economic function as paramount, the others do not.

A number of the "functional" theorists assert that deferred consumption is what saving is all about. In other words, people are not making choices between saving now and spending now, but between spending now and spending later. Probably the best known of these is Friedman's (1957) Permanent Income Hypothesis. This claims that people have expectations about their income across their lifespan and so have an idea of their underlying "permanent income". If income in a period is more than this they will save it; if it is less they spend from savings. These kind of theories are all firmly based on a model of a rational economic being who is making choices between various consumption patterns; x now and y later or a now and b later.

Similarly based on rational economic models are those theories that assert that people save for interest. Keynes argued that interest was not important as a reason for saving. This is still contentious although most empirical studies have found that interest has no effect at all on saving (e.g. Boyle & Murray, 1979) or even that higher interest rates reduce saving (e.g. Weber, 1975). Katona (1975, p.244) uses survey data to claim that although interest rates do not affect the amount people save, they do affect the kind of savings they hold. But even if the rate of interest is not an important motivation for saving, it still has significance for other theories. A higher rate of interest, for example, would mean that less saving was needed to provide for future consumption under the lifecycle hypothesis.

Theories that don't emphasise economic function but assert that saving can be a goal in itself are found in both economics and psychology. Clower and Johnson (1968) maintain that wealth (which is after all in most cases accumulated savings) should be treated as an independent source of utility. Katona (1975), rather similarly, maintained that an adequate reserve of money (i.e. savings) is a consumer good like a washing machine or a pair of skis. People will aim to "acquire" this reserve in the same way that they aim to acquire consumer durables as they become more wealthy. Children presumably are less likely to require a rainy day reserve (after all, what are parents for) but wealth could still have a value over and above its purchasing power. There might, for instance, be some status to be had from having a large sum in a saving account.

A rather different kind of perspective on this issue is found in psycho-analytic theories, especially those of Freud (1908/1959) and Ferenczi (1914/1976). The essence of their approach is that faeces are the first property of the child and thrift is derived from the pleasure of retaining faeces (and spending from the pleasure of expelling them). Thus the kind of anal eroticism the child displays (retentive or expulsive) will affect the adult character: Saving is a descendant of anal retention and will vary according to personality type. Here saving is just a form of hoarding.

In addition, to these theories, there are a number of generalisations from demographic data that suggest other influences on adult saving. A number of factors are known to affect saving, such as income level, wealth, age, social class and the state of the economy. Unsurprisingly, people with a higher income are more likely to save than poor people (Koskela & Viren, 1983), although they are just as likely to "dissave" as anybody else (Katona, 1975). Again, as one might expect, the middle aged save more than retired people or young adults (part of this difference is the result of income and wealth). More interesting is the effect of social class. There is a long tradition, from Weber (1904/1976) onwards, of identifying the middle classes as the repository of the work ethic, entrepreneurial drive and savings. Results from both surveys and experimental work on delay of gratification provide complementary evidence. Freire, Gorman, and Wessman (1980) showed that working class subjects tended to have a shorter time-perspective and valued smaller rewards that became available immediately rather than large rewards that were only available in the future. This type of data was used as evidence to support the notion that the working classes were more "impulsive" and so less "rational' than the middle classes, but, as Sonuga-Barke (1988) suggests, rationality can be defined in many different ways, and a preference for immediate rewards can be a rational response to an uncertain future (Logue, 1988).

SAVING FROM THE SOCIO-DEVELOPMENTAL VIEWPOINT

During our discussions of the development of children's saving in the following chapters we turn again to the relationship between functional and non-functional understandings of saving. We will argue that different periods during development, as well as different economic theories, can be distinguished in terms of functional and non-functional understandings of economic activity in general and saving in particular.

From the socio-developmental child-centred view adopted in this book, saving is an activity with both functional and formal aspects. Consequently we are interested both in the way the child comes to take on a particular view of the legitimacy of certain economic goals and intentions relating to future consumption, and the way those intentions are fulfilled by the practical actions of the child.

On the formal level saving is defined in terms of the quality of a set of actions (going to the counter and depositing money) made in relation to one or other institution (bank or building society). From the functional point of view saving is a problem-solving exercise; more specifically it is an adaptive response to the income constraint problem. Constraints on personal income are a necessary restriction on the choices people make. The fact that money spent on items in the present cannot be re-spent in the future leads to an inclusive relationship between present and future consumption. Thus when assessing the cost of each choice alternative the value of the future choices that an individual might make should be taken into account. When a child wants an expensive toy, and is given small amounts of money regularly, saving involves a series of choices in favour of the desired deferred reward. Offers of less valued toys or sweets must be resisted if the child is to be able to buy the most desired toy. During saving, the period of time between a choice and its consequences is not a direct time cost, because subjects are free to behave in any way they wish during that period. For example, if you put one hundred pounds under the mattress for safe keeping, there is no need to mark the passage of time, patiently sitting by the bed, while you wait to enjoy the rewards of thrift. In fact, the reward is often much sweeter if you forget that the money is under the mattress, so that on returning, there is an element of surprise in finding that you are one hundred pounds better off, and can pay for the leaking pipe to be mended after all. What *we* call saving here is always voluntary but may be discretionary or contractual.

CHILDREN'S SAVING: THE EXISTING LITERATURE

Our interest in children's saving must at the very least be based on evidence that age related changes in levels or form of saving do occur during childhood. But does such evidence exist? In a study carried out over 30 years ago, Dickins and Ferguson (1957) found that both intentions to save and successful saving increased with age. The majority of the children in both of their age groups (7 and 11) said that they were saving for a special purpose, with Christmas presents being the most common target. Ward et al. (1977) report very similar findings; most of their (much bigger) sample saved and were saving for particular reasons. Again, saving increased with age. What both of these studies ignore is that saving increases with income and since older children generally have more income they will generally save more. Two recent British studies do, however, show clear age differences in saving. Furnham and Thomas (1984) found that older children saved more than younger children and also they saved for different reasons and in a different way. The older children used savings accounts. Tysoe (1983) also found a surprising number of children with savings accounts (60% of her 10 year old subjects) and comments on the surprising degree of economic sophistication shown by these children.

So it appears that levels of, and interest in, saving do change as a child grows. But are these changes simply due to older children having more money or more ready access to the "technology" of saving? Or is there something more fundamental going on?

Research into delay of gratification provides a partial answer to this question (Pressley, 1979). If given a choice between a small reward that they can have immediately or a large reward for which they must wait, young children generally choose to have the immediate reward while older children choose the larger delayed reward (Mischel & Metzner, 1962). Clearly the ability to delay gratification increases with age. More importantly for us, this ability seems to go hand in hand with an increasingly sophisticated understanding of the practical problems inherent in delay of gratification and of the effectiveness of the strategies used to complete the task (Mischel, 1981; Mischel & Mischel, 1983), e.g. strategies that reduce the tempting qualities of the small reward, such as thinking about other things or hiding the reward (Mischel, Ebbensen & Ziess, 1972). Might the increased understanding and use of strategies that aid delay of gratification also be at the heart of the increases in levels of saving that occur as children grow?

With regard to this, while it is clear that children must learn that choices between present and future consumption are difficult to make (i.e. they must have some understanding of "temptation" and related problems) and that there are a variety of saving strategies (including institutional ones) that provide effective solutions to these problems, delay of gratification and saving are not equivalent situations. Experiments on delay of gratification test childrens' waiting rather than their saving ability. The time before the delayed reward becomes available is essentially wasted time. The child has to sit and wait for the reward in an experimental chamber, and sitting and waiting is the price of the delayed reward (Sonuga-Barke, Lea, & Webley, 1989; Sonuga-Barke, Webley, & Lea, 1989;). In a saving situation, by contrast, an individual is not restricted in this way while delaying consumption—delay does not constitute the cost of the large reward. The situation used in Mischel's studies also differs from a typical saving situation, as Mischel's subjects had only to make one choice between small immediate and large delayed rewards, whereas in a saving situation a series of choices need to be integrated over time.

The strategies that were effective in the delay of gratification paradigm, then, might not be effective when applied to saving. But clearly there are certain similarities between the two situations. Each saving "response" does require "impulse" control. So these strategies may aid saving behaviour in particular situations. For instance a child who is saving up for a bicycle and is confronted with a sweetshop might look away, cross over the road or think about anything but the taste and sticky satisfaction of eating sweets. Or the money might be put in a piggy bank or a savings account, using one of the formal strategies that have been developed to aid saving behaviour.

Apart from age changes in saving and "self control", the literature does give some information about class-differences. Newson and Newson's (1976) study of the world of English 7-year-olds, for example, found that middle-class children received less pocket money (18p compared to 30p) but saved a far greater proportion of it over a week (90% compared to 48%). In other words the majority of the working class children spent all their money within a week. This result may be distorted by self-presentational concerns on the part of the parents and is not confirmed by the two American studies of Goldstein and Oldham (1979), and Ward et al. (1977), although this may reflect a genuine difference between the two cultures. Ward et al. do report that there were social class differences in the long term saving of 13-year-olds.

One way to look at these differences is to see them as related to differences in child-rearing practices or economic behaviour within the family, which might pose different types of economic problems for children. Children from working class backgrounds may not be taught to place such high value on distant, and perhaps uncertain rewards, as children from more affluent and economically stable homes. It is not that these children are less able to produce effective temptation inhibiting strategies but rather that they do not get the opportunity to do so.

OUTLINE OF THE STUDIES TO FOLLOW

In this book we are interested in the way the child comes to express economic identity in terms of the legitimate and desired ends of economic behaviour, in the process of transmission of those ends from adult to child, and in the way the child learns to construct the practical means to those ends by solving the problems posed by the types of economic constraint previously discussed. In Chapter 3 the psychological correlates of the changes in performance that lead to the development of adaptive economic behaviour under income constraint will be studied. These studies will be carried out in a fairly abstract way using board games. Chapter 4 will involve a more wide-ranging look at the way children understand the functional and formal aspects of saving and related topics. In Chapter 5 the wider social context in which children save will be studied using a content analysis of advertising literature from the savings institutions and interviews with parents about their attitudes to their children's saving. In Chapter 6 we will put forward a speculative explanation of the results of all these studies. In Chapters 7 and 8 we give Anna Emilia Berti, and Shlomo and Sharone Maital, all eminent scholars in the field, the chance to comment on our thesis. In Chapter 9 we reply to the criticisms and comments and re-present the basic principles of the socio-developmental approach in the light of them.

3 The Development of Functional Saving in a Play Economy

THE DEVELOPMENT OF SAVING AS A RESPONSE TO INCOME CONSTRAINT

In the preceding chapters, we introduced the concept of functional saving as a response to income constraint. When the cost of a desired item of consumption exceeds levels of income, combining income over a period of time allows that item to be bought. This saving requires the integration of a series of choices between present and future spending. In this chapter, three experiments will be described in which children attempted to solve this type of income constraint problem in a play economy.

Three Precursors to the Development of Functional Saving

It could be argued that before a child's saving can be considered as a truly functional response to income constraint the child needs to fulfil three developmental conditions.

First, they must understand the inclusive nature of all choices under such a constraint. The realisation that such choices are made, not between spending and not spending, but between spending now and spending in the future is at the root of the development of saving. If saving is not based on an understanding that buying in the present restricts future spending we cannot really talk of a child saving in any purposeful sense.

It is generally conceded that carrying through a decision to provide funds for future consumption by saving is difficult. Boehm-Bewark (1891, p. 253), an early economist, wrote that, "It is one of the most pregnant facts of experience that we attach less importance to future pleasures and pains, simply because they are future and in the measure that they are future". More recently, Maital (1982, p.54) has echoed this sentiment; "The pervasive preference for a certain and immediate dollar, or half penny, over a delayed future one—time preference in economist's jargon—is an apparently permanent fixture in human society."

Economists like Boehm-Bewark, Maital and others such as Irwin Fisher (1930) first represented people's preference for present goods over future goods in terms of the psychological erosion of the value of future goods. Psychologists such as Mischel (1958), have also argued that there is a form of "natural" impulsiveness that might prevent people from integrating consumption over time (see also Ainslie, 1975). Given this, it is clear that children need to learn ways of making sure they carry through their decision to save. On a practical level this involves the development of the ability to use strategies.

The idea that the development of a strategic component is crucial to the development of competence is not of course unique to the field of saving (Wellman, 1985). It has been used in connection with the development of a number of other abilities, e.g. memory (Brown & Barclay, 1976; Fabricius & Wellman, 1984; Kennedy & Miller, 1976), and "self control" (Mischel, 1981; Mischel & Mischel, 1983). The major argument in each case has centred around the concept of meta-knowledge (Flavell & Wellman, 1977). Meta-knowledge is the understanding a child has of his or her own abilities (Schnieder, 1985) in relation to the difficulty of the task in hand (Wellman, 1977), as well as of the effectiveness of the strategies available to complete that task (Kruetzner, Leonard, & Flavell, 1976).

So two other types of understanding are required for the development of functional saving. It is not sufficient for the child just to appreciate the inclusive nature of choice. First the child must also have an understanding of the concept of "temptation" (where temptation acts as a general expression of the difficulty of choosing between present and future consumption) as well as other sorts of threats such as theft. Second they must understand that "saving" strategies provide effective ways of solving these problems.

In modern times, adults' saving has become institutionalised, with savings banks offering a wide range of saving plans for different people in different circumstances. These formal strategies are available to children and appear to be used by a large percentage of them. These methods of saving have the advantage of also giving interest. But strategies need not be formal. Children are presented with choices between spending and saving in situations where institutional forms of saving are not available. In these situations informal strategies similar to the temptation inhibition ones found to be effective in delay of gratification studies might be used.

To summarise the list of precusors to purposeful saving: (1) the child must understand the inclusive nature of economic actions, and so realise that choices are made not between spending and not spending but between spending now and spending in the future; (2) the child must develop a realistic understanding of his or her own abilities to save in the face of the range of problems economic life brings; (3) the child must develop a realistic understanding of the role of strategy as an aid to solving the difficult problem of providing for the future.

The first two experiments presented in this chapter examine the relationship between these precursors and the development of functional saving during children's attempts to solve the income constraint problem in play economies.

STUDY 1: CHOICES UNDER INCOME CONSTRAINT

The First Play Economy: The Players

Sixteen girls, four at each age studied (4, 6, 9 and 12 years) took part in the study, in a room in the Psychology Department at the University of Exeter.

The Equipment

Figure 3.1 shows the arrangement of apparatus in the play economy room. The table, on which the board game was to be played, was positioned in the centre of the room. The board game used in Study 1 is shown in Fig. 3.2. To one side of this was a lever pressing machine (which rewarded children for respones on two levers with small brass tokens).

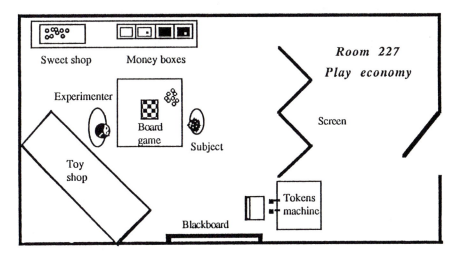

FIG. 3.1.   The arrangement of the apparatus in the play economy room that was used in Studies 1, 2 and 3.

A "toy shop" and a "sweet shop" (at which these tokens could be spent) and a "bank" (at which the tokens could be saved) were also placed around the table. The bank consisted of four savings boxes each representing a different combination of physical and psychological characteristics. These characteristics were varied along two dimensions:

1. Facilitation or inhibition of impulsive behaviour. Work by Mischel and co-workers (see Pressley, 1979 for a review) has shown that the amount of attention directed to a "tempting" stimulus is an important determinant of a child's ability to delay gratification. Strategies that limit the levels of this attention facilitate "self control". In the present experiment subjects were given the choice between boxes with clear perspex doors and those with solid wooden doors.

2. Long term or short term commitment. The role of commitment in effective "impulse control" has been stressed by a number of researchers (e.g. Rachlin & Green, 1972). Subjects were given the choice between banks offering different levels of commitment. Tokens could be withdrawn after a complete circuit of the board from some boxes; from others they could be withdrawn on a number of occasions during each circuit. Table 3.1. shows the particular characteristics of each box.

Alongside the lever pressing apparatus was a blackboard upon which each subject's "tokens score" was recorded. Each of these facilities (except the lever

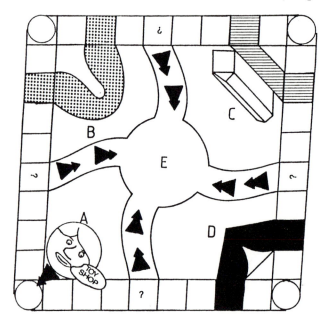

FIG. 3.2.   The board game used in the first play economy. A represents the Toy Shop; B represents the Robber; C represents the Sweet Shop; D represents the Tollgate and E represents the Bank.

TABLE 3.1
Description of Savings Boxes

Box Nos.	Physical Characteristics	Psychological Characteristics		
		Commitment	Flexible	Temptation
1	no access/clear	long term	no	enhancing
2	no access/covered	long term	no	inhibiting
3	access/clear	short term	yes	enhancing
4	access/covered	short term	yes	inhibiting

Physical characteristics determined psychological characteristics. Tokens could not be withdrawn from those boxes designed to give long term commitment (inflexible) as these boxes had no means of access. Those boxes designed to give a short term commitment (flexible) allowed subjects access to tokens through a flap door during each board game circuit. Clear boxes had a transparent perspex front panel—covered boxes had solid wooden front panel.

pressing apparatus and the blackboard) was represented by a square on the board game. The board game also had squares that represented a robber and a toll gate.

The Rules of the Game

Each circuit started and ended on the square directly preceding the first "bank" square. Before the start of each circuit of the board, subjects spent 15 minutes earning tokens on the level pressing machine. Each child took part in three once-weekly sessions. Each child made a total of three circuits around the board. During the game subjects were only allowed to move from one square to another after they hit a target with a ball. Subjects always travelled around the board in a clockwise direction one square at a time. This method ensured that the problems were presented in a constant order.

The long term goal of the game was to save enough tokens to buy a toy from the toy shop. These toys were divided into four price categories. So that the children could understand this classification each price category was colour coded. The most expensive toys were coded green, the next most expensive were coded red, the next blue, and the least expensive yellow. The average price of the toys in the green price category was approximately five pounds sterling. The total number of tokens was recorded on the blackboard, which was divided into 200 squares numbered from 1 to 200. The group of squares associated with a particular price code were filled in with the appropriate colour, so that squares 1 to 24 remained black, squares 25 to 74 were coloured yellow, squares 75 to 124 blue, squares 125 to 174 red, and squares above 175 green. The pricing system was explained to the children in terms of these colour groupings. The number of tokens earned by a child on the level pressing task was marked off by filling up the appropriate number of squares on the blackboard with ticks. Each token lost or spent by the child resulted in the removal of a tick from one square. This ensured that the child could keep a clear record of her gains and losses as she moved around the board.

Children were given the chance to use a particular facility only after they reached the associated square of the board game. When the child landed on the square associated with the sweet shop, she was given the opportunity to buy sweets. Four varieties were available at the sweet shop. Each sweet cost one token. Similarly, children landing on the square representing the toy shop were given the opportunity to buy a toy. In addition, children lost one token when they landed on the square acting as the robber, and had to pay one token to pass the square representing the toll gate. The squares representing the "bank" were positioned in between each of the squares representing the other facilities. Access to the bank was arranged so that each subject had the opportunity to use the bank to solve the specific problem with which she would shortly be faced. For example, a child landing on the "bank" square situated before the square associated with the robber could deposit all her money in the "money boxes" and thus prevent the robber from stealing it.

Introducing the Game to the Players

On her first entry into the experimental room, the child was asked to sit down next to the game board. She was then asked. "When you go shopping with mummy what type of shops do you see down town?" After the child had answered, the experimenter would say "You see this board in front of you, it is arranged so that there are all the shops and things that you will find when you go shopping with mummy. You see there is a sweet shop, a toy shop, a bank, robber and a toll gate (ferry lady)". The child was then asked if she understood what all these things were. If the children were unsure of the meaning of any of these things, the experimenter took some time to explain them. After these explanations, the experimenter said to the child, "We are going to play a game on this board. In this game you can go the sweet shop, the toy shop and the bank, and across the toll bridge, if you land on the robber square the robber will take one penny. The pennies that you will use in the game you will earn on the machine over there." The experimenter pointed to where each of these was situated, while at the same time relating them to particular squares on the board. After this was done, the child was guided around the board and asked what would happen if she landed on each of the squares on the board.

Questioning the Players During the Game

At specified intervals around the board the children were asked a series of structured questions. More detailed discussion of both these questions and the answers elicited can be found in the results and discussion section. The answers to these questions were tape recorded.

The experimenter kept a complete record of all the economic transactions made during the child's passage around the board, including the number of visits made to the bank (for both withdrawal and deposits), the position on the board at which these visits were made, the savings box chosen by the child, and the amount of money both stolen from and spent by the child.

RESULTS

What the Players Did

Table 3.2 shows the children's performance on the board game. The success of a child's economic performance on the board game was measured by adding tokens spent on sweets, and tokens taken by the robber, over the three circuits. Both the number of tokens spent on sweets and the number of tokens stolen showed a significant decrease across age groups ($F=3.57$, $d.f.$ 3, 12, $P<0.05$). When subjects' performance was compared over three circuits there was found to be no significant practice effect ($F=1.09$, $d.f.$ 2,24, NS).

How did this change relate to changes in other dependent measures?

The Average Size of Sweet Purchase. The total number of sweets purchased was divided by the number of purchases. Although suggestive, the significance of the finding of no age differences in this measure was difficult to determine given the wide variation in the number of times children of different ages actually bought any sweets.

The Number of Visits to the Bank. There was no significant change in this dependent measure with age ($F=0.39$, $d.f.$ 3,12, NS).

The Use of the Deposit Facility of the Savings Boxes. The total number of times subjects had all their tokens in one or more of the savings boxes when they

TABLE 3.2
Combined Performance in Study 1 on Eight Dependent Measures for Each Age Group

Behavioural Measure	Age			
	4 yrs.	6 yrs.	9 yrs.	12 yrs.
Money stolen	10	9	1	1
Money spent	53	25	16	5
Total lost	63	34	17	6
Total trips to the bank	22	18	23	25
Total deposit before robber	2	3	11	11
Total deposit before sweet shop	1	2	10	10
Total withdrawals before toll gate	2	0	6	11
Average size of sweet purchase	4.8	2.7	4	5

passed the robber and the sweet shop were compared. This is a measure of the functional use of the savings boxes. A significant increase in both of these dependent measures occurred between the ages of 4 and 12 years (F=11.82, *d.f.* 3,12, P<0.01; F=19.53, *d.f.* 3,12, P<0.01).

The Use of the Withdrawal Facility of the Savings Boxes.   A third measure of effective use of the savings boxes was the number of withdrawals made from the bank just before the toll gate, ensuring safe passage across the river. There was a significant increase in this dependent measure across ages (F=8.09, *d.f.* 3,12, P<0.01).

Choice of Savings Boxes.   Figure 3.3 shows the subjects' preferences for the different savings boxes. Overall there was a strong preference for the boxes offering regular access to tokens. There is also an increase in preference for box 4, (with solid wooden doors) and a decrease in preference for box 3 (with the perspex door) between the ages of 6 and 9.

What the Players Said

In the introduction to this chapter, three precursors to the development of functional saving were specified. The child must have understood the *inclusive* nature of choice under income constraint, that these choices were often difficult to make and that the savings boxes provided some assistance in helping to carry through the difficult choices.

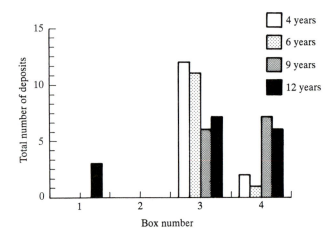

FIG. 3.3.   The number of deposits into each of four "banks". See Table 3.1 for descriptions of the characteristics of the four banks.

The Development of an Understanding of the Inclusive Nature of Choices Under Income Constraint.   Subjects displayed an understanding of the inclusive nature of choices when they recognised that spending money had consequences for choices in the future. In order to test this, two separate questions were asked each time the child lost tokens. The first of these was, "What has changed now that you have lost those/that token(s)?". The second question was "What is bad about that?"

It was not enough for children to say, as Patty (4) did, that "If I spend my pennies I have to get some more". They also needed to show that they understood that this change affected the availability and quality of future choices. An example of such an understanding would be Claire's (6) comment that "If I spend my pennies on the yellow I won't be able to buy the blue one". Only after both these type of statements had been made by the child could it be said that she had developed an understanding of the inclusive nature of economic action. None of the 4 year olds showed any understanding of inclusivity, three of the 6 year olds did, and all of the 9 and 12 year olds did.

The Difficulty of Carrying Through Choices to Save.   Although no questions were specifically asked of the children about this topic, for fear of influencing the amount of sweets bought, none of the 4 year olds or 6 year olds mentioned the problems encountered at the sweet shop. Three 9 year old subjects gave the possibility of being tempted by the sweets as the reason for either leaving or putting their money in the bank.

The Role of the Saving Strategy.   The children's understanding of the savings apparatus was examined by asking them about their motives for saving at the different banks. An acceptable level of understanding was indicated if, when landing on the savings square before the robber the child said, as Gail (9) did, that "I'll put it in to make it safe from the robber", or on landing on the savings square before the toy shop "I won't take it out of the bank as I don't want to be tempted" (Mary, aged 9).

None of the 4 year olds showed an understanding of the role of the savings bank in either context, whereas all of the 9 and 12 year olds did in both contexts. The 6 year old group was intermediate; none understood the savings box as a strategy to prevent succumbing to temptation, two of them understood that it gave protection.

DISCUSSION

The most significant improvements in performance on the board game occurred between the ages of 6 and 9 years. This was not due to older children using the banks more than the younger children, or to them buying less sweets on each visit to the shop (these measures were essentially constant over the range of ages) but rather was related to a number of differences between younger and older childrens' scores on other behavioural and verbal dependent measures.

First, older children's use of the banks was more often functional. This is shown by the increased number of saving responses made either to the threats posed by the robber or temptation of the sweet shop, as well as by the increased use of the withdrawal facility before the toll gate. Older children lost less tokens in these situations. Unlike those from the younger age groups, these subjects displayed an understanding of the difficulties faced when choosing between immediate and future consumption. This understanding was articulated in the form of statements about "temptation" as well as through the increasing preference for the covered savings boxes, which were designed to attenuate temptation. At this age children also understood the role of saving strategies, so that saving in the "bank" before the sweet shop was associated with an understanding of "temptation", and in the case of the bank before the "robber", it was associated with an understanding of the economic consequences of being robbed.

In comparison, the performance of the 4 and 6 year olds could be described as prefunctional. At age 4, the randomness of saving responses was matched by a total lack of any attempt to explain the reasons why one should save or the effects of saving. For instance, when asked why she used the saving boxes, Patty (4) replied, "Because I do; because I did it before."

Although by the age of 6, subjects seemed to understand the inclusive nature of choices under income constraint, there was nothing to suggest that they had developed an understanding of either the problems encountered when making such choices or the role of saving strategy. Their poor performance on the game suggests that, as suspected, an understanding of the inclusive nature of choice, although logically necessary for saving, is not sufficient for the development of effective saving.

Some Contradictions in Performance During the Prefunctional Years

There are some interesting contradictions in the performance of the 6 year olds. The first was between what they said about saving and what they did. On the one hand they seemed to regard money saved as money lost. This was well expressed by Sarah (6), when she said "If I put my money in the bank I won't have any left". Beth (6) and Catherine (6) also showed this confusion. When they were asked if they wanted to use the money boxes they both replied "I don't because I'm saving up".

On the other hand, despite telling the experimenter about the negative economic consequences of saving and that it served no economic purpose, these children did save. While 6 year olds did deposit money as often as the older children a lack of understanding of the function of saving was also evident from the profile of deposits. They occurred in situations where they could serve no economic purpose. All this suggests that they appeared to value saving, but they did not define that value in terms of its economic consequences. So what did determine the value of saving for the 6 year olds?

Although no questions were asked specifically about the virtues of saving, it became apparent through their spontaneous statements, that the 6 year olds had been informed of its merits by their parents (many parents later confirmed this observation). They did understand its significance as an act with meaning on the social level, although they saw no value in saving as an economic practice.

This suggests that 6 year olds' understanding of saving as a social act plays an important role in determining behaviour during these prefunctional years. Children appear to have been taught the value of saving as a social practice but not its function. This view is also supported by the way that these children talked about the threat posed by the robber. Rather than explaining it in terms of threat to their stock of tokens, subjects explained the action of the robber in terms of its social characteristics; as Beth said "Oh no not that naughty man again".

STUDY 2: SAVING—A RESPONSE TO DIFFERENT TYPES OF THREATS

In Study 1, children aged 9 and 12 years made functional use of the bank in both temptation-threat and theft-threat situations. As all subjects understood the threat posed by the robber, this suggests that the developments in understanding temptation paralleled those in the understanding of the function of the savings boxes. But studies on the development of memory and other cognitive skills show that younger children have great difficulty in realistically assessing their abilities to perform even simple tasks (Kail, 1979; Miller & Bigi, 1977). Given this, one might expect that the understanding of the strategic significance of the savings box might precede the understanding of temptation unless: (a) the use of "savings bank" is a particularly difficult strategy to learn. Young children might associate possession of tokens with their safety. In Study 2 children's use of the "savings bank" was compared with an intuitively more simple "saving" strategy; a "detour", which was available to circumvent the threats posed on the board game; (b) saving responses under temptation-threat in Study 1 were facilitated by the robber being presented to the child before the sweet shop. In Study 2 this order was reversed; (c) the intensive questioning of subjects about their motives to save and their understanding of saving had specific effects on savings performance. In Study 2 the number of questions asked was restricted.

In addition to these changes in design, a measure of resistance to temptation was constructed based on an assumption that underlies many quantitative accounts of temptation. This is that the relative preference for a small immediate reward over a large delayed reward reverses as a function of absolute delay to the two rewards (Ainslie & Hernnstein, 1981; Rachlin & Green, 1972; Strotz, 1956).

Two squares before the sweet shops subjects were asked to predict the number of sweets they would buy. These predictions were then compared with the size of the actual purchase, and the percentage of actual sweet purchases predicted was calculated. From this we could work out the extent to which the childrens' initial plans of consumption changed over time as they were faced with the "tempting" situation.

The Second Play Economy: The Players

Twenty four girls participated, eight from each of the age groups studied (6, 9, and 12 years).

The Equipment

The apparatus differed from that used in the first study in three ways. First, a different board game was used. Second, small, brightly painted, wooden figures were introduced to signify the different actors in the game (a bank manager, a sweet shop owner, a toy shop owner and a robber). Third, movement from one square to another was determined by the throwing a white square on a dice, which had three white and three black squares.

The Rules

Before the start of each circuit, subjects spent 15 minutes earning tokens on the lever pressing task. Each subject took part in one session that lasted approximately two and a half hours during which time she made three circuits of the board. As in Study 1, the long term goal of the game was to save enough tokens to buy a toy. The number of tokens saved was recorded on the blackboard and the same colour to price code was used.

The board game used is shown in Fig. 3.4. It differed from the one used in Study 1 in a number of ways. There were two sweet shop squares and two robber squares while there was no square representing a toll gate. The number of tokens "lost" on the robber squares was increased to four, although the price of sweets was the same as in Study 1.

As in Study 1, four squares gave access to the savings boxes. In addition, four others gave entry to or exit from the two detours. The position of the "savings box" squares corresponded to the "detour" entry and exit squares in terms of distance from the sweet shop or robber squares. The same savings boxes were available at the bank. Entry into the detours and access to the "savings box" was contingent on the child providing an explanation of their use. This was done to reduce the possibility that the detour facility was used randomly. Apart from this, no other questions were asked of the children. When subjects landed on the square marked "count" the experimenter removed any money that was in the bank and handed it back to the child to count.

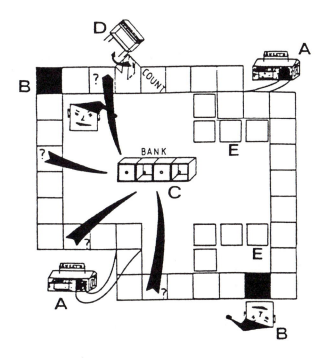

FIG. 3.4. Board game used in Study 2. A represents the Sweet Shop; B represents the Robber; C represents the Bank; D represents the Toy Shop & E represents the Tollgate.

At the start of the game subjects were introduced to the board game as in Study 1. The only difference was that after the subjects had been introduced to the game, they were asked to specify their favourite toy from the toys in the shop.

RESULTS

What the Players Did

A number of behavioural dependent measures are summarised in Table 3.3.

Total Spending. The number of tokens spent at each of the two sweet shops was compared across ages and over circuits. While there was a significant decrease in the number of sweets bought ($F=10.82$, $d.f.$ 2,21, $P<0.01$), there was no effect of the position of the shop ($F=0.06$, $d.f.$ 1,21, NS). There were no significant practice effects when performance was compared across sessions ($F=2.38$ $d.f.$ 2,42, NS).

Losses by Theft. The tokens robbed by each of the two robbers were compared across age groups. Again there was a significant effect of age

TABLE 3.3
Combined Performance During the Second Play Economy on 10 dependent variables

Dependent Variable	Age		
	6 yrs.	9 yrs.	12 yrs.
Money stolen	100	52	40
Money spent	374	104	23
Total trips to bank	46	39	40
Total deposits before robber	0	11	15
Total deposits before sweet shop	0	4	13
Use of detour before the robber	20	24	23
Use of detour before sweet shop	7	9	15
Average size of purchase	14.1	4.5	3.8
Percentages of sweet purchases predicted	56%	45%	30%

(F=12.60, d.f. 2,21, P<0/01). In addition, significantly more tokens were lost to the robber near the banks than to the robber near the detour (F=61.61, d.f. 1,21, P<0.01). There was also a significant interaction between the position of the robber and age (F=3.99, d.f. 2,21, P<0.05). Taken together these measures suggest that there were significant age related improvements in performance.

The Number of Visits to the Bank. As in Study 1 this measure was approximately equal across age groups (F=0.26, d.f. 2,23, NS).

Measures of the Functional Use of the Savings Box. The number of times subjects had all their tokens in the bank when they passed the robber and when they passed the sweet shop were compared. There was a significant increase in functional responses with age (F=15.44, d.f. 2,21, P<0.01). Overall, there were significantly more saving responses made under theft-threat than temptation-threat (F=9.80, d.f. 1,21, P<0.01). There was also a significant interaction between the nature of threat and age (F=6.2, d.f. 2,21 P<0.05). Saving responses under theft-threat contributed significantly more to the total responses than those under temptation-threat in the 9 year old group. Figure 3.5 shows the total number of times the savings boxes were used effectively by children at each age.

The Use of the Detour. The number of times subjects used the detour to by-pass the robber was compared with the number of times it was used to by-pass the sweet shop for each age group. No significant increase in the use of the detour occurred (F=2.32, d.f. 2,21, NS), although the detour that by-passed the robber was used significantly more by children of all age groups (F=21.18, d.f. 1,21, P<0.01) Figure 3.6 shows the total effective use of the detour facility by children at each age.

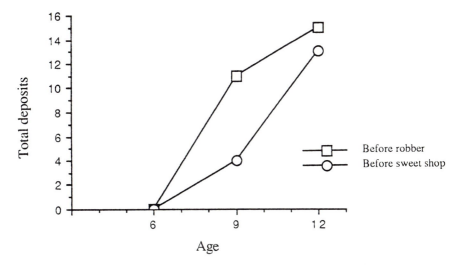

FIG. 3.5.   The mean number of times the saving strategy was used effectively by children in each of the age groups when faced by temptation and theft threat situations.

The Average Size of Purchase.   There is a decrease in average number of sweets purchased, with the major reduction occurring between the ages of 6 and 9. Because of the variation in the number of visits to the sweet shop across ages, this data does not give strictly independent information and so, although suggestive, is not suitable for statistical test.

Measure of Resistance to Temptation.   The percentage of each child's actual sweet purchases predicted was compared across ages. There were a number of different circumstances under which responses were classified as "no prediction": (a) if the child had no tokens to spend; (b) on some occasions subjects would not make a prediction; (c) on some occasions the predictions made were too vague to be included. The number of predictions made decreased across age groups. There was no improvement in the accuracy of the predictions with age. This suggested that the older children were no better at "handling" temptation when they got to the sweet shop than younger children.

Type of Box Used.   Figure 3.7 shows the subjects' choice of savings boxes for each age group. As in Study 1, subjects preferred boxes with regular access, but were indifferent between the clear or covered boxes. Subjects showed an increasing preference for the clear limited access box (A) and a decreasing preference for the clear regular access box (C) with age. Preference for the other two boxes remained constant.

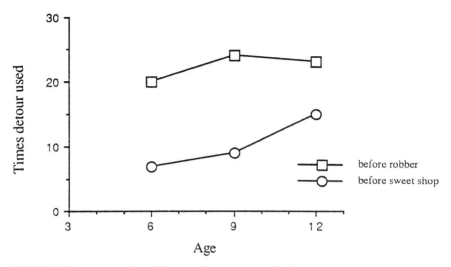

FIG. 3.6.   The mean number of times the detour was used effectively under both temptation threat and theft threat.

What the Players Said

The only two questions asked during the study were, "Why do you want to go to the bank", and "Why do you want to go to use the detour" ("this road")? Again the explanations given by the 6 year olds were phrased in language that referred to social/moral rather than economic consequences. The answer "Because I do, because it's good" was characteristic of such responses. The social, rather than the economic, significance of these actions for these subjects, was also suggested by the spontaneous statements about the robber. Anita (6) said "If I spend all my money on sweets the robber won't be able to get them". By this gesture she forfeited more tokens than were due to the robber. Valerie's (6) statement that "If I lose my tokens the robber won't be able to get them" also supports this point.

DISCUSSION

The Development of Saving as a Response to Theft-threat and Temptation-threat

The results of Study 2 support and extend the findings of Study 1. Significant decreases in money lost during the game were again related to changes in the profile of saving behaviour and its functional use rather than absolute levels of saving. The relationship between the development of a functional saving ability and improvement on the board game could also be seen in the fact that older children were no better at predicting actual levels of sweet purchase than younger

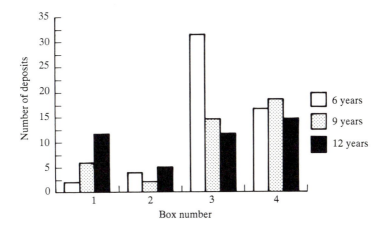

FIG. 3.7.   The number of deposits into each of the four banks. See Table 3.1 for the characteristics of each bank.

children. Children from all age groups underestimated the number of sweets that they would buy. Immediate rewards had an equally potent effect, when covaried with sweet preference across all age groups. Less "damage" was done to the older children's stock of tokens than the younger children's, partly because they faced the tempting stimuli less often (i.e. they adopted effective saving strategies) and partly because they liked sweets less than the younger children (the average size of the sweet purchase did show a recognisable decrease across ages).

As expected, the changes introduced to the experimental design had the effect of separating the developmental paths of saving in temptation-threat and theft-threat situations. The 9 year old subjects, unlike the 12 year olds, made a significantly greater number of functional responses in theft-threat than in temptation-threat situations. This result suggests that the 9 year olds understood the functional significance of the savings boxes, while not yet understanding the difficulty posed by the "tempting" stimulus at the sweet shop. This point is reinforced by the finding of wide discrepancies between the use of detour under these different types of threat. Children from all age groups, even the 12 year olds, used the detour to by-pass the robber more often than to by-pass the sweet shop.

STUDY 3: CHOOSING BETWEEN ACTIONS WITH SOCIAL OR ECONOMIC VALUE

The results from Study 1 suggested that the way children understood the value of economic actions changed as they grew. While the younger childrens' understandings were defined in social/moral terms those of older children were defined in terms of economic consequences. In Study 3 we aimed to provide an explicit test of this view.

Subjects played a board game during which they had to choose between a "socially" neutral course of action (paying a toll at a river) that had negative economic consequences (loss of six tokens) and an action defined in negative social terms (being robbed) that had more positive economic consequences (loss of only four tokens). In Game 3 choosing the socially neutral alternative had a negative effect on the child's financial well-being. If social definitions of value do play an important role in determining young children's economic behaviour then the young children (6 year olds in this study) should choose the alternative with positive social characteristics, irrespective of negative economic consequences.

In addition, two aspects of saving were studied. First, the effect on saving of experience of an equivalent activity, hiding, was studied. Hiding money, unlike saving, is not part of the specific social vocabulary of thrift, and consequently the instructions to hide do not possess the same moral overtones as instructions to save. Despite this, hiding money is similar in a number of ways to saving money. Both require the loss of physical control over money and both can be regarded as possible strategies to avoid loss of money in the theft-threat situations. It is possible then that experience of the benefits of hiding money might help translate 6 year olds' frequent though non-functional saving responses into effective saving behaviour.

Second, the child's understanding of temptation (i.e. the difficulty of making choices between present and future rewards) was studied in greater detail.

The Third Play Economy: The Players

Ten boys and ten girls from each of the ages studied (6 and 12 years) took part in the study.

The Equipment

The board used for Study 3 is shown in Fig. 3.8. Although the sweet shop was removed from the game all the other items present in Studies 1 and 2 were also present in the play economy in this experiment (toy shop, lever pressing task, money boxes and blackboard). There were four robber squares, one positioned at each corner of the board, whereas there were no squares representing the sweet or toy shops (the toy shop, although still found within the play economy, was not represented on the board). In addition there was no square representing the bank. These squares were replaced by two other squares; on one was written the word "save" and on the other the word "hide". These two squares were each positioned an equal distance from a robber square. The two squares that had the word "get" written on them were used for the retrieval of the money that had been saved or hidden. In order to test for the effects of hiding on functional saving, only half of the subjects at each age received the opportunity to hide their money (the "hide" condition). For those that did not (the "no hide" condition) the word "hide" was covered up with a thick piece of white card. As in Study 2 there were two detours. Unlike that study, both these detours could be used to circumvent the robbers. These detours also differed from those in the last study in that passage along them required a river crossing (by boat). This crossing was contingent on the payment of a toll.

The Rules

Before the start of each board circuit subjects spent 20 minutes earning tokens on the lever pressing task. Each subject took part in one session that lasted approximately two and a half hours during which time they made three trips around the board. As in Studies 1 and 2 the long term goal of the game was to save up for a toy. In this study no price to colour code was used for different categories of toys. Instead, each child was set a tokens target. This was represented by a star positioned within the appropriate square on the blackboard. The children had to earn a certain number of tokens by the end of

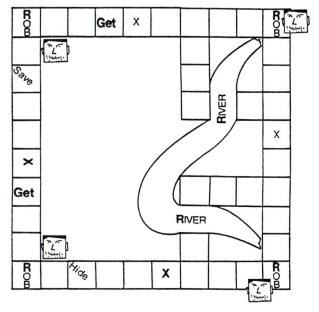

FIG. 3.8.   The board game used in Study 3. "ROB" represents the robber: "Save" represents the opportunity to save tokens: "Hide" represents the opportunity to hide tokens: "Get" represents the opportunity to get hidden or saved tokens back. "X" represents the point at which questions were asked. "River" represents the point at which the ferry was available to detour around the robber square.

the third circuit if they were to be given "their" toy. Failure to reach this target resulted in a child being awarded a small consolation prize.

Four tokens were lost each time a child landed on the robber square. The size of the toll varied from river to river. At one river it was two tokens, at the other it was six tokens, so that at one the children were given the choice between being robbed of four tokens or paying a toll of six tokens whereas at the other corner they were given the choice between being robbed of four tokens or paying two.

Half of the subjects at each age arrived at the cheap ferry first whereas the other half encountered the more expensive one first. The children were asked a number of questions as they passed around the board. These questions are printed in Table 3.4.

What the Children Were Told About the Game

When the children entered the room they were told:

> "In the game you are about to play you will have the chance to win a toy of your choice. You can do this by earning pennies on the machine over there" (experimenter then points at the lever pressing tasks) "when you have earned some pennies you will bring them over here and put them on the game board. This game is a bit like Ludo. Do you know how to play Ludo? The most important thing to remember when you play this game is that there are four robbers" (experimenter then points to the robber squares).

The experimenter then asks the question; "Do you know what a robber is? Do you think that he is a good or a bad person?" After the children answered this question they were told that the robber "steals four of your pennies". The experimenter continued:

> "But there is another way that you can go, (the experimenter then points to the river) if you go this way you can go across the river on the boat. It is important to remember that to go across this river on this boat (experimenter points to one of the detours) will cost you two pennies while to go across the river at this point (experimenter points to the other detour) will cost you six pennies."

TABLE 3.4
The Questions Asked of the Subjects During Study 3

1   Can you name two things that you would find tempting?
2   Why are these things tempting?
3   Is it good or bad to be tempted?
4   Imagine that there was a plate full of sweets in front of you and you had not eaten for a whole day so that you are very hungry, but your mummy said that you could not have any of the sweets. How would you stop yourself taking the sweets?

After this the experimenter went on to discuss what all the other squares meant. At the end of this subjects were asked to describe what would happen if they landed on different squares on the board. Finally subjects were reminded that any pennies that they lost on the board game would be removed from their score and so would affect their chances of winning their desired toy.

RESULTS

Social or Economic Definition of Value

The choices made by the subjects between the robber and the ferry are summarised in Table 3.5. The results were analysed using a three-way ANOVA. There were three independent measures. Age and sex were between subject factors and "cost of ferry" was a within subject factor. The performance, collapsed across circuits, was used as the dependent measure. This analysis showed that boys and girls chose in similar ways ($F=0.19$, $d.f.$ 1,36, NS). But there was a significant effect of "cost of the ferry" ($F=92.77$, $d.f.$ 1,36 $P<0.001$) and age ($F=50.37$, $d.f.$ 1,36, $P<0.001$), as there was a significant interaction between "cost" and age ($F=30.54$, $d.f.$ 1,36, $P<0.001$). These results suggest that improvement in economic performance with age was due to older children choosing the cheaper alternative more often than the younger children irrespective of whether it was "offered" by the robber or the ferry lady.

TABLE 3.5
The Choice Made in Favour of the Ferry

Age	6 yrs.		12 yrs.	
Cost of Ferry Crossing	2	6	2	6
Boys				
Circuit 1	10	7	9	1
Circuit 2	10	7	9	1
Circuit 3	10	7	9	1
Girls				
Circuit 1	10	9	8	2
Circuit 2	10	9	10	0
Circuit 3	9	8	10	0

The choice made in favour of the ferry as a function of cost of the ferry for subjects of different ages and different sexes

Saving and Hiding

As in Studies 1 and 2 the measure of the functional use of the savings box was the number of times each subject deposited all their tokens in the savings bank. Likewise the measure of functional hiding was the number of times each subject hid all their tokens from the robber. Tokens were considered hidden if some effort was made to place the tokens out of sight of the robber.

Table 3.6 shows the total number of functional responses made on both saving and hiding squares for subjects at each age group, under both the hiding and the saving conditions. The data was again analysed using an ANOVA. Age, sex and whether or not there was an opportunity for the children to hide their tokens, were between subject factors. The dependent measure was the number of saving responses on all three circuits. Only the interaction between the presence of the hide facility and age was significant (F=11.64, $d.f.$ 1,16, $P<0.05$). Taken together these results suggest that experience of hiding helped the children to produce effective and functional saving responses.

TABLE 3.6

The Total number of Functional Hiding and Saving Responses for Subjects in Each Age Group

Age	6 yrs.		12 yrs.	
	Hide	Save	Hide	Save
Boys				
"Hide"				
Circuit 1	3	3	4	4
Circuit 2	4	4	4	4
Circuit 3	4	4	4	3
No "hide"				
Circuit 1	–	1	–	3
Circuit 2	–	1	–	3
Circuit 3	–	1	–	3
Girls				
"Hide"				
Circuit 1	1	1	4	4
Circuit 2	1	1	4	4
Circuit 3	2	1	4	4
No "hide"				
Circuit 1	–	0	–	1
Circuit 2	–	1	–	1
Circuit 3	–	1	–	1

Children's Understanding of Temptation

The children were asked a series of questions about what they understood by the term temptation and how they might resist temptation in their everyday situations.

1. All of the 12 year old subjects identified two things that they found tempting. This was usually some form of food such as sweets. One of the more unusual items that were recorded was "pinching my sister". A large number of the 6 year olds could not identify tempting things. It appeared that they didn't really know what it meant to be tempted.

2. Those 6 year olds who understood the term tempting and could name things they found tempting were asked why these things were tempting. The replies given by the subjects can be divided into three types. One group of subjects isolated the "impulsive" component of a tempting situation. For instance David (6) said that "you feel so hungry that you can't stop yourself". A number of subjects concentrated on the consequences of being tempted. For instance Mark (6) said "mummy might tell you off". A third group were far less specific and simply reported that it was related to some kind of emotional state. For instance Ray (6) reported that "it's like angry" and Mike (6) said "it makes you quite cross . . . fed up".

As would be expected the 12 year old subjects' explanations were more sophisticated and complete. For instance Fay (12) said "When someone tries to encourage you to do something that is nice but bad" and Doris (12) said "it may be nice but it is wrong". Both of these understandings express quite clearly the conflict that temptation brings. This conflict of interest is perhaps best summed up by Catherine (12) when she said "you want to do something that you don't want to do".

3. The questions about whether it was a bad or good thing to be tempted did not lead to many satisfactory answers. Most subjects at both age groups, when pushed, thought it was a bad thing. The older children accepted that its value was conditional on the nature of the object of desire. For instance Fay again said that "it is bad if it costs a lot".

4. Questions about the strategies that would be used to avoid temptation produced the greatest number of replies. There were distinct difference between the replies of different aged children. The strategies reported by the 6 year olds can be divided up into two groups. Those that involved either eating something else or trying to get their mother to give them some of the sweets, and those that involved moving to another physical location. The first type of approach is that taken by Mike (6) when he said "I'd try to take some but my mum might see me". The second approach was adopted by Sue who said "I'd go somewhere else". John had a rather complicated approach to this problem; he said that "If I try to take some, I get sent up to my bedroom and then my mum calls me and I say that I don't want it any more".

The responses given by the 12 year olds were all of the same sort. Their strategies did not involve moving to a different location, rather they reported that they would employ different kinds of ideational strategies. All of the 12 year olds mentioned that their strategy would involve "thinking". For instance Claire (12) said that "I would close my eyes and think of all different things" and Mike (12) said, "I would thing about the consequences of taking it".

DISCUSSION

In this study we examined the way that younger children's understanding of the value of action affects their economic performance. Six year old subjects of both sexes showed a preference for the ferry crossing even in those situations where they lost more tokens to the ferry than if they had been robbed by the robber. On the other hand, the 12 year olds preferred the alternative that resulted in the smaller loss of tokens, whether this was associated with the ferry crossing or not. Consequently the 6 year old subjects lost more tokens at these corners of the board than did the 12 year olds. This coincides with the findings of Studies 1 and 2. This loss of tokens can be seen as the direct result of children adopting definitions of the value of economic actions based on social representations rather than economic consequences.

In this study 6 year old children valued actions that led to them escaping the robber more than those that led to them retaining their tokens, whereas the 12 year olds valued the alternative that led to them keeping the most tokens possible.

Turning to the effects of practice of an equivalent activity, hiding, on saving, the results suggest that using the "hide" facility encouraged the use of the "save" facility. Making functional hiding responses increased the number of functional saving responses made. In Study 2 it was reported that only the older children spontaneously referred to temptation as a reason for using the savings box. This suggestion is supported by the finding that very few 6 year old subjects actually understood the meaning of the word temptation. But when asked to imagine a situation in which they would be tempted, a number of subjects could in fact think of good strategies to avoid temptation. The answers given to the questions about temptation suggest that an understanding of more sophisticated temptation-inhibiting strategies developed as the children grew. The trend can be summed up as going from behavioural strategies, like moving away from the stimulus, to cognitive strategies, like thinking about something different.

THE DEVELOPMENT OF SAVING REVISITED

In the introduction to this chapter we suggested that the ability to adapt to income constraints, through saving, is essential to the fulfillment of the personal economic aims of Western societies when income is limited. We suggested that, in essence, this depends on understanding that outcomes of choices taken in the present affect the choices available in the future. In practice, because of the problems that choosing between immediate and delayed reward presents, the effective translation of this understanding into behaviour requires two other developments. The recognition that a preference for immediate reward is normally a powerful determinant of choice, and a knowledge of strategies that allow a decision to save to be carried through effectively.

After carrying out the three experiments reported in this chapter we can see the emergence of a clear, but quite involved, picture of the main developments that occur as children become effective economic actors and produce functional saving behaviour. We can see that only 12 year olds produced truly functional saving behaviour. They used the bank more often in situations where saving served an economic function. They also described their saving in functional terms. In contrast, 6 year olds saw saving in the banks as serving no useful function. Some even reported that saving had negative economic consequences. But these children made frequent and indiscriminate use of the banks and so exhibited high levels of non-functional saving.

These changes in behaviour did appear to correspond to changes in the way children understood the nature of intertemporal choice and effective strategy. Those over 6 years of age appeared to understand the consequence of spending now on the possibilities for spending in the future. Not until the age of 9 did children understand the role that the savings boxes could play in moderating the threat posed by the robber, and not until the age of 12 did this understanding of strategy combine with an understanding of the power of the tempting stimuli to determine choices, although children as young as 6 appeared to have some understanding of the nature of tempting things. By the age of 12 the bank was used by children to protect their money from themselves.

On a different level the development of functional saving coincided with changes in the way that the children defined the value of saving in the bank. It appeared that the younger childrens' notions of value were determined on the social level, a view supported by Study 3, and were categorical rather than functional, whereas for the older children they were based on economic consequences. From the socio-developmental viewpoint these changes in the way that the children understand the value of their economic actions are viewed as significant. Indeed the fact that 6 year olds combine a non-functional and indiscriminate saving style, a view that saving is a bad thing in an economic sense, and a "dogmatic" understanding of the value of saving based on the psuedo-moral assertions of their parents, suggests they are perhaps the main determinant of the high levels of observed saving.

In Chapter 5 we will return to look again at the social aspects of the child's understanding of saving and then go on in Chapter 6 to outline an account of the role that these types of factors might play in the development of effective saving.

4 Extending the Boundaries of the Play Economy

INTRODUCTION

The studies described in Chapter 3 were of a fairly unrealistic nature. In Chapter 4 we assess the extent to which the account of the development of functional saving presented so far can be said to characterise developments in "real world" saving.

THE STATUS OF THE BOARD GAME PLAY ECONOMY

Certainly the assumptions underlying the suggestion that the board game economies used in the first three experiments were in some way "models" of the actual economy raises a number of different issues. Were we insensitive to the participants perception of the experimental situation? This would have a number of implications for the way the results of the study should be interpreted.

First, it was unequivocally a "game". A game that the older children in particular might have found a bit "beneath them". Second, the board game may have presented economic problems that the children would never face in the real world. Income constraints, although very real in the adult world may not be significant at all in the child's world. Parents may buy children all they need. Third, it may require the subject to participate in a particular "game playing" style. If so it becomes dangerous to generalise about children's capacity for functional behaviour in the real world. In order to overcome these problems, the play economy used in the next study was rather different. While recognising that

43

an accurate reproduction of reality is not possible, we set out to create an environment that allowed the children greater flexibility and that we hoped would encourage them to construe the "artificial" economy in a more realistic way. Essentially we provided information that allowed the children to construct a "play economy reality" and so gave them the opportunity to tell us about the significance, function and meaning of saving in their day to day lives.

Through this game, with its very real options (eg to spend money in a sweet shop or spend time in a video arcade) we provided a salient environment in which participants could be asked about the real life equivalents of the situations presented. In other words the participants understandings of the play economy were used to gain access to beliefs and behaviours so difficult to study with children in real life situations. The importance of the participant's own understandings meant that the notion of an "external threat" posed by a robber had to be discarded. It is not possible to integrate a believable robber into a realistic play economy.

INSTITUTIONALISED SAVING

In this chapter we will also look more closely at the distinction between personal/private saving in a piggy bank or money box and institutionalised/public saving with banks and building societies. In the previous studies we found that some young children believed that money saved was money lost. It could be argued that this could have been a result of the practice of parents initiating contractual saving at high street banks and building societies on behalf of their children.

In order to provide a fuller understanding of children's saving we need to distinguish between the experience provided by contractual saving initiated by parents and carried out at the bank, and piggy bank saving initiated by the child and carried out at home. Given that children have experience both of money boxes and banks it is not reasonable to conflate the two.

The "bank" (presented as a way of dealing with external threat and internal temptation) used in the first three studies did just this. It was in fact a set of four money boxes, which varied in significant characteristics. There is a large conceptual leap in moving from a choice of money box to the child's use and understanding of real banks.

So in this study a distinction was made between saving in a money box and saving in a bank. Institutionalised saving was differentiated by ensuring that it took place in a different and distinct environment and in a realistic way, with paper financial transactions. Money boxes were employed only in the home environment. Normally use of a "bank" would require some prior knowledge, but in the present study the actual behaviour in relation to the bank is not as important as the opportunity to interview the child *in* the bank environment about their understanding of banks and bank-related strategies.

THE RELATIONSHIP BETWEEN THE DEVELOPMENT
OF SAVING AND CONSUMER STRATEGIES

In Chapter 3 we studied the way children used formal saving strategies, e.g. depositing money in a savings box. In this chapter we will look in more general terms at how children's styles of consumption relate to their growing ability to save. If one focuses on consumption style a rather different picture of the development of saving might emerge. We all need ways (like saving, hiding, having no money in our purses, using coins and notes for different purposes, allocating money from particular sources to particular expenditure) to cope with liquidity of money and our inability to resist temptation and external threats but there need be no developmental hierarchy of beliefs about the best strategies to use. Furthermore, it may be the case that childish strategies solve the childish problems quite adequately, even if they appear inferior.

STUDY 4: MONEY MANAGEMENT IN A MORE
NATURALISTIC SETTING

The Fourth Play Economy: The Players

Thirty 6, 9, and 12 year old boys, 10 from each age group, (who were recruited from local state schools) took part in the play economy, which was spread over a set of four rooms.

The Play Economy

Figure 4.1 shows the arrangement of rooms in this play economy. Room 1 was double the size of the other three (approximately 20′ by 10′). This housed the "Home", "Toy shop" and "Bank". In the "Home" corner there was a coffee table (with books, a pot plant and some paper on it) and three easy chairs. On the wall there was a poster and a notice saying HOME. In the "Toy shop" corner there was a chair and table. On the table were between 15 to 20 toys. On the adjoining wall were stuck three toy posters and a notice saying TOY SHOP. There was a fair variety of toys displayed; e.g. a kite, some Lego sets, model planes, model cars, remote controlled model vehicles, books, board games etc. These were chosen to appeal to boys of the age range studied. The price of these toys was not marked (their average cost in the shops was £3.80 with a range of £1 to £7). In the "Bank" corner there was another large table with a swivel chair behind it and a notice on the wall saying BANK. On this table there was some paperwork, a black metal strongbox and four money boxes. These were given by three building societies for their young savers (The Halifax—a plastic house; Anglia—a plastic orange teddy; Abbey National—a cardboard house) and a Pooh "Munny box" (a cardboard cylinder).

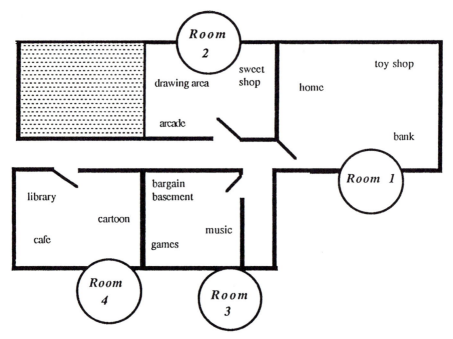

FIG. 4.1.   The arrangement of rooms used in the second play economy.

Rooms 2–4 each contained three activities. In each room one activity cost 10 tokens (a day's pocket money), one activity was of variable cost and one was free. Room 2 housed the video arcade (10 tokens), the sweet shop (variable) and a drawing area (free). The video arcade consisted of a BBC computer with several standard games available (e.g. Space Invaders). The sweet shop was a medium sized table with a minimum of 30 different kinds of sweets on it e.g. Maltesers, crisps, chocolate bars, Smarties. The drawing area was a corner of the room with a good quality drawing pad and crayons. Each area of the room had an appropriate notice on the wall behind it and, in addition, the drawing area had drawings on the wall.

Room 3 housed the Music area (10 tokens), the bargain basement (variable) and indoor games (free). The Music area consisted of a cassette player and headphones with a choice of story and pop music tapes. The bargain basement was a small round table with a wide assortment of cheap items on it, e.g. packets of balloons, dice, toy animals, gummed paper shapes, stickers, pencil sharpener, pirates eye-patch etc. The indoor games area was a corner of the room with a half-completed 100 piece jigsaw and a pack of cards. Each area of the room had an appropriate notice on the wall.

Room 4 housed the Cartoon show (10 tokens), the Cafe (variable) and the Library (free). The Cartoon show consisted of a video machine with Tom and

Jerry cartoons. The Cafe was a small table with an assortment of drinks in cans and bottles. The Library had approximately 30 books displayed, suitable for the age of the participants and able to be read in the time available (e.g. Asterix books, *Guinness Book of Records*). Again, each area of the room had an appropriate notice on the neighbouring wall.

The Rules of the Economy

A series of semi-structured interviews were carried out with questions being asked at appropriate times during play. Before we describe these questions we need to explain the essentials of the way the economy functioned and the way it was explained to the child.

Passage through the economy was divided into five main periods. At the start of the experiment the economy was explained, the child chose a target toy (cost 70 tokens), was issued with a library card and opened a bank account (with a "start up" gift of 30 tokens). In the first "three day cycle" the child visited each of the rooms for 10 minutes in turn, returning "Home" to get his daily pocket money (10 tokens). In the Bank period the child was given the opportunity to deposit or withdraw money from his account.

In the second "three day cycle" the child again visited each room in turn for 10 minutes, again returning home for his daily pocket money, and in the concluding cycle the child was able to withdraw money from the bank and buy a toy. The child was given 90 tokens over the period of the game. He had to save 70 of these if he wished to take home his chosen toy. If he failed to save enough, he was able to buy a less desirable toy.

A typical session would go as follows: After the child had been settled (this involved a cursory look into all the rooms) he was introduced to the economy while sitting in the "Home" area of Room 1. The economy was explained as a speeded up week, where each day would last just 10 minutes.

> Just as in a week of the school holidays, there are different things to do each day and it is possible to choose what to do each day. The activities available might be things you would find if you went into town—or maybe things that you would do at home instead. Some activities will cost money, some more than others. In order to be able to pay for these, you will get 10 tokens of pocket money each day. Regardless of how much or how little you spend, every day you will get 10 tokens of pocket money. The only thing you have to do is spend one day (in other words 10 minutes) in each room before you return here. For each day you will be able to choose from three things; one will cost 10 tokens, one will cost nothing and with the other you can spend a little or a lot, whatever you like. The game will last for six "days" so you will visit each room twice. It will be like going from Monday to Saturday with Sunday off.

Before the game actually started there were a number of things that the child had to do. First they had to select a toy that would serve as their goal in the study.

After the child had chosen a toy he was told that "in order to take that toy home you will need to have 70 tokens left over".

The chosen toy was then displayed on the high stool and the bank account was opened. It was explained that a parent or grandparent had decided to open an account for them and that all they had to do was decide where they would like this account to be held. This they did on basis of their preference for a particular money box which they could take "Home". It was carefully explained that there were 30 tokens in the account to which they could add (or take away) after three "days" and at the end of the "week". The 30 tokens were entered into a personalised bank book and were never actually seen: as in a real situation, the transaction was a paper one. It was then explained that "the Bank will be available if you want to use it again at the end of the third day, after you've spent one day in each of the rooms".

When this exchange was complete, the experimenter and the child returned to "Home" for a final run-through of the game. The child was again told how much money they needed before they could buy the toy and that a bank was available for their use. Then the first day's activities were described and the first day's pocket money distributed. Children were given frequent recaps as to the workings of the game.

Before entering each room the child was asked to look at the notice on each door (which described the activities available) and to make his choice. If the 10 token activity was chosen the experimenter took the money: if the variably priced activity was chosen the child was asked how much he believed he might spend. At the end of 10 minutes the child and experimenter returned to "Home" where the next day's pocket money was given.

At the end of the game, if the child had saved enough tokens, he was able to buy his chosen toy. If he had not got enough tokens, he was able to buy a less desirable toy.

The Questions

Questions were asked at the various stages of the game. All conversation between the experimenter and the child was tape recorded and later transcribed. Questions were not asked in a standard form but were tailored to the individual child. Thus, particularly for the younger children, the same question might be asked in a variety of ways and sometimes more than once.

During the introduction to the game the questions were factual in nature. The information that was sought included: (a) whether the child received pocket money and, if so, how much. This was asked when the function of pocket money in the play economy was explained; (b) whether the child had a money box and how much they had in it. This was asked when the money box was being chosen by the child; (c) whether the child had a bank account and, if so, if they had access to it, how often they used it, who opened it and how much was in it. This was asked in the bank area, again to emphasise the reality of the bank.

As well as being of general interest this enabled us to draw parallels between the play economy and the real world. During the first three day cycle no questions were asked while the child was engaged in the activities available in the rooms. However, the time when pocket money was handed out was used to extend the experimenter-child dialogue. Between day 1 and day 2 the child was asked about their economic relationship to their siblings and parents. The relationship between the amount of pocket money received and the cost of presents was explored. Between day 2 and day 3, the theme of budgeting was explored and the role of saving and money boxes was explored, e.g. what, in a typical week, would pocket money be used for?

The opportunity to use the bank came at the end of the third day. In the bank the transactions chosen by the child provided an ideal opportunity to ask questions about banks in general:

1. What is the best/worst thing about banks?
2. Is saving in a bank the same as saving in a money box?
3. If you had a choice of where to put your money, where would you put it (and why)?

During the second three day cycle no specific topics were explored, but the familiarity of the child with the options available and the closeness of the end of the game did lead to various topics being discussed. On some occasions, this included some attempted negotiations for more tokens from the experimenter or a reduction in the price of the chosen toy.

At the end of the game it was possible to examine the behaviour of the child, the repercussions of his behaviour, the strategies used by the child to overcome the problems posed within the economy. The discussion also included questions on: What does saving mean? What are banks? Is it a good thing to save and if so, why? Why save in banks? Is it difficult or easy to save? Why? Does everybody find it that easy or difficult?

Before the game ended the child was asked about his understanding of the play economy and his beliefs about it. For example:

1. Why did we have a bank in this game?
2. What did you think the experiment was about?
3. Was it boring or interesting?
4. What was the best thing about the game?
5. Was it what you expected before you came?

RESULTS

In the introduction to this chapter it was pointed out that the income constraints presented in the board game studies in Chapter 3 might be unrepresentative of the type of problem that children face within the context of their families.

What is clear from discussions with the children in this study is that they do engage in complex saving and spending strategies each and every day of their "economic" lives. But as none of the children had financial independence (only one 12 year old had a part time job) their parents play a crucial role in determining how much money is available and how that money is handled. Parents have an acknowledged veto over many possible strategies available to children and are instrumental both in setting up and carrying out the economic strategies that their children use. No subjects were old enough to have open access to their money in any institution and none could get to it without the knowledge of their parents.

This implies that we have to acknowledge the possibility that parents can modify the actual economic demands of situations facing children (an issue not studied in Chapter 3). A number of subjects suggested ways in which this might happen. Some subjects suggested that their parents would "top up" any money that the child had managed to save so that a prized toy could be afforded. Others suggested that they did not save at all because their parents can, *in extremis*, always be relied upon (e.g. to buy a sibling's birthday present). This makes a *spend, spend, spend* strategy perfectly reasonable, not to say rational. Others suggested that they did not save weekly pocket money because the larger blocks of income from birthday money, grandparents etc are adequate for all larger items wanted.

On occasions this approach to money management was translated into a "play" strategy and used in the present study. One child realised that he had overspent about half the way through the game. He discussed with the experimenter the possibility of receiving some help and a price for a cheaper toy was finally agreed (a new target). The child proceeded to overspend a second time. This led to a second set of less successful negotiations. What is interesting is that he felt able to be lax in his spending, safe in the knowledge that some suitable compromise would be reached.

Children who saved but who had not made sense of the Bank may well also have believed that the experimenter would help them out; that some willingness to save on their part would be matched by some generosity on the part of the experimenter. This all implies that saving cannot be considered in isolation and has to be considered within the context of the child's social and economic relationships.

Even given this evidence that parents can moderate the demands of the economic environment, we can still be confident that for many children, (particularly those older children engaged in large scale consumption) the income constraint problem presented here and in Chapter 3 is very real indeed. There are very few parents who are a "bottomless pit", while the desires for consumption of the latest fad, be it "He Man" or "My Little Pony", will always outlive the patience and generosity of most parents. Or in other words saving does serve a function for most children in our society when they are young and will be an essential skill for good housekeeping when they have access to finances themselves.

THE CHANGING UNDERSTANDINGS OF SAVING; FORM AND FUNCTION

Now we can turn to the development of children's understandings of the form and function of saving observed in this more naturalistic setting. We will highlight the performance of each age group separately.

Six Year Olds: Their Economic Style and Understanding of Saving

Six year old boys performed poorly in this setting. None of them had enough money saved by the end of the "week" to buy their desired toy. Regarding their style of economic action during the "week", many 6 year olds either made no attempt to save, spending their money at will, or saved by default, i.e. spending only half their money.

Those subjects who didn't save appeared to have little thought for long term goals and the effects current spending would have on later spending opportunities. It was enough in itself to be able to consume the sweets, drinks, toys or whatever in each room. The lack of concern for the future was expressed by one 6 year old;

"I might spend half, I might spend all my money".

"I might spend all of it accidentally because I don't know how much things are".

All the subjects who adopted this approach claimed that they had tried to save and indeed some did make token efforts, usually on the last day. But all seemed happy to be let loose in the sweet shop or cafe, and even if they remembered the need to save this didn't affect the way in which they allocated their finances between one activity and another or between the present and the future. Attempts to save by spending only half appeared to be based on a vague idea that if you don't spend very much money you ought to have sufficient left over at the end to reach your target. Generally this meant buying one item from the variable price option each day. One child said;

"I'm only going to buy one thing a day . . . so I'll still get some money to put in my money box."

If this strategy were followed rigidly it would lead to overspending but it can still reasonably be described as an attempt to save, since it was maintained even after the point of no return had been reached (i.e. after the child had spent more than 20 tokens). As in the studies described in Chapter 3 it seemed that children at this age understood the role of the savings bank in essentially non-functional terms. For instance, one of the children said;

"cos I've not spent it on things that cost 10 and I put the rest in here" (*indicating money box*).

This was also apparent in the reasons given for their choices. The Anglia was chosen because "I like the bear's eyes", "I like the honeypot". The Halifax was chosen because "it's easy to open", "it looks like a house and you can put the money in the back" and "because it was a proper moneybox".

As in Study 1 some 6 year olds not only failed to grasp the function of saving, but they thought it had bad economic consequences. Three children spoke of saving with banks as being analogous to losing their money. Although when questioned about the role of banks generally, they said that banks were for saving, only one of the three thought it might be a good idea, in economic terms, to save with banks.

But this understanding of saving was restricted to saving with banks, which was seen as different from saving in a money box. One of the boys expressed it like this:

E: Do you think it is a good idea to put money in banks?
C: Yes so the bank people can look after it instead of your money box.
E: Is it the same to put money in your money box as it is to put it in the bank?
C: No . . . because you still might be able to get it in the money box, but you won't be able to get it in the bank.

This suggests that this child believed that you ought to put money in the bank, even if you don't like it, because it is "good". There is also a recognition that when it is the bank we are free from temptation. The other two children saw saving as losing quite explicitly:

E: Do you think putting money in a bank is a good thing?
C: No
E: Why?
C: Cos if you spend all your money up, you need to get some more.
E: Can you get some more from the bank?
C: No.

Here putting money in the bank is equated with spending it. Banks are perceived as institutions that take money without giving anything in return. The next child had a similar view.

E: Would you put money in the bank?
C: No.

E: Why not?
C: Because I want to save it.
E: When you put money in the bank what happens to it?
C: You lose it and they give you a tiny bit of money back.

This belief is not unreasonable, given that a child does not have access to money in a bank or building society and that decisions taken to put money in banks will be taken by parents and not by themselves. The lack of a functional understanding of saving was also exhibited by two 6 year olds who said they preferred bank saving to money box saving. This preference centred around the fact that saving in the bank was "rewarded by extra money" or interest.

E: What happens to your money if you put it in a bank?
C: You get interest.
E: How much interest do you get?
C: It depends on how much you put in there.
E: Why do you get interest?
C: Cos they . . . thank you, so, cos you lent them your money for a long time and you get interest back then.

(The idea that interest is a bank saying "thank you" is found in some banks' promotional material). The second child who talked about interest did so in a more oblique fashion. Indeed, the term "interest rate" was not mentioned.

E: Do you think it is better to put your money in a money box or a bank?
C: In a bank cos, if like I had about £20 in the bank, they would save up about 50p, cos in my bank I've got £12.50 and I put £12 in—
E: How did that happen?
C: I don't know.
E: So how do you think that 50p got there?
C: They saved up.

The appearance of extra money is understood through his own experience. To have more money you must save, therefore the bank must have saved. This may make the bank a particularly good place to have money since they are better at saving than you are. It appeared that saving in the bank was seen as different from saving at home. Much of the money in banks and building societies comes from birthdays, Christmas etc. and is placed in accounts where it is, to all intents and purposes, inaccessible. The money in these accounts was generally quite a significant sum. When asked if they would withdraw it and spend it if they could, most children said that they couldn't conceive of circumstances where they would need to use the money. They would ask their parents for anything they needed that was expensive and possibly receive it as a birthday present. The money in their account was consigned to the long term future, being there to buy a car or pay for University.

Some of the 6 year olds did exhibit a primitive understanding of the function of the savings apparatus. Some saw it as a handy place to put money so that you could remember where it was. This was exemplified by one child:

E: Why did we have a moneybox in this game?
C: So I wouldn't lose any of my money.
E: When you put your money in the box were you saving it?
C: No, it was for my pocket money.
E: When you put money in the bank, was that saving?
C: Yes

Others saw it as a way of keeping money safe from other people.

E: Why do you put your money in a moneybox?
C: To keep it safe
E: Safe from whom?
C: ... people might get it

This idea of an external threat was also relevant to children's choice of moneybox. Several children chose the Abbey National box because they thought the hole (for putting coins in) was less detectable and therefore less likely to be seen as a money box if thieves broke in. Saving to deal with external threat will be further discussed in the next section, as 9 year olds also employ this idea.

Nine and Twelve Year Olds Economic Style and Understanding of Saving

Overall seven of the 9 year olds and nine of the 12 year olds were successful (the unsuccessful 12 year old was almost successful, saving 66 tokens). These older boys adopted various approaches to the task in hand.

Saving by not Spending at all during the Game. This strategy was used by only two 9 year olds but both gave interesting justifications for it. One child seemed intent on not spending even though he said afterwards that he didn't think he could save up enough to get his target toy (he had not included the 30 tokens in the bank in his calculations). Why then did he bother to save? It is possible that he saw the whole object of the game as a test of his ability to deal with temptation, but more likely, given the comments and behaviour of other children, that he believed his attempts to save would be rewarded by the experimenter making up the difference. This is reasonable as it is a common occurrence in the real world (a child saves towards something and the parent makes up the difference).

The other child spent nothing either even though he had calculated at the outset how much he could spend and recognised during the game when he had saved enough. He seemed to get extra pleasure out of doing things that were free, as though this, in itself, conferred more value on them.

Saving Up until Target Reached and Then Spending.   One 9 year old used this strategy, which involved not spending during the first "three day" period and then spending on the second circuit when the 70 tokens required had been obtained. This was not a utility maximising strategy since it meant not paying for a go on the video arcade, which was thought overall to be the most attractive option. The boy referred to this approach as "making sure that I was safe".

Calculated Saving.   This strategy was used by three of the 9 year olds and eight of the 12 year olds. It involved making calculations at the beginning and deciding what to spend the discretionary 20 tokens on. This was explicitly stated to the experimenter and usually meant paying twice for either the video arcade or the cartoon show. Some children didn't spend on the first day (just to get the hang of the game) and then made their calculations.

It is worth noting that children making these careful calculations construed the game in the way the experimenter intended; as a "saving" game. It would often have been more "lucrative", given the prices of the chosen toy and activities within the game relative to their real world prices, to spend as much as possible during the game.

Spending only half.   Two of the 9 year old children adopted an approach to the game that was very much like those used by half of the 6 year olds. They spent half of everything that they had, holding onto the vague belief that they would be left with enough to buy the toy of their choice.

In addition to these general approaches to the economy we isolated five main understandings of savings employed by 9 year olds: (1) saving by forgetting; (2) the institutionalisation of saving; (3) saving as safety; (4) saving as a protection against external threat; (5) the bank as a forced saving strategy.

Saving by Forgetting.   A number of the 9 year olds mentioned that both banks and money boxes were good for saving because you could forget about the money you had. All except two children thought that saving in a bank was better than saving in a money box but those who talked about the latter gave it an interesting role:

E: Does a moneybox help you to save money?
C: Yes, cos you can forget what's there.

A moneybox helps because out of sight is out of mind. Another child had a more active approach:

E: If you were saving up, how would you do it?
C: I'd try and save up and keep it in my money box and forget about it and once mum gives me some more money, put it in my moneybox and forget about it again.

These short term strategies seem to be safeguards against a lack of self-control.

The Institutionalisation of Saving.   It is clear that for 9 year olds banks and financial institutions are beginning to be bound up with their constructions of saving.

E: Do you think it is a good idea to save?
C: Yes.
E: Why?
C: It's better than keeping it in your pocket.
E: Do you think it is hard for everyone to save?
C: Not really, cos all you have to do is put it in the bank.

Increasingly, to save means to use the bank. This is made explicit by this boy:

E: Do you think it is a good idea to save?
C: Yes, cos if something cost £2, then you can get it out the bank.

Saving as Safety.   As with some 6 year olds, several 9 year olds used considerations of the safety of their money. These notions of safety were applied equally often to the bank and the money box. One child differentiated between kinds of saving but saw both bank and money box as safe:

E: What do you think banks are for?
C: For keeping your money safe.
E: Do you think it is better to put your money in a bank or money box?
C: In a bank, because in there it is safer. If I get £5 for my birthday that's the money I put in the bank.
E: Do you put your pocket money in your moneybox?
C: Yes, cos you wouldn't lose it . . . you wouldn't lose your money.

So banks are safer but a money box keeps money from being lost.

Saving as Safety from Others.   Keeping money safe from external threat was also important.

E: How would you explain banks to someone who had never heard of them?

C: You can have an account and get money out and put money in, you can have cheques. You can put money in and the bank looks after it so it doesn't get stolen.

It is likely that most of the money stolen from children is taken by siblings who are quick to claim ownership if money is not carefully looked after. The most explicit reference to a perceived external threat came from one child who was concerned over his money's safety if it wasn't in a bank:

E: Wouldn't it be better if I just kept it? (rather than put it in a bank)

C: No, cos a pocket stealer could steal it.

Bank as a Forced Saving Strategy.   This child saw bank saving as good because of the external discipline and commitment it imposes:

E: If you had a choice between putting your money in a bank or in a money box, where would you put it?

C: In a bank, because they make you keep it open.

E: How would a bank make you save better?

C: Because if you take it *(money)* in a bank, you've got to keep *so much* money in there.

Along with these themes raised by our 9 year olds some other themes emerged from discussions with the 12 year old group: (1) interest rates; (2) safety of money (from self); and (3) the explicit recognition of the parental role in saving.

Saving as Earning Through Interest.   This issue was never raised by the experimenter during conversations and all references to interest rates were made by the boys themselves. Nonetheless, all 10 of the 12 year olds offered "interest rates" as their primary reason for putting money into a bank. Interest rates were invariably raised in response to the question "What is the best thing about a bank?". On one occasion, interest rates were brought up in the introduction, a boy saying "Can I ask if there's any interest in this bank?" When interest rates were offered as the best thing about banks the children were questioned further on their understanding of them. Interest was described as:

"You get more, eh, you get added on amounts to the amount you've got in."

"Well you earn interest on your money I suppose. It gets bigger by a couple of quid a week I expect."

"Well, if you put so much in, they invest it somewhere else and you might think that they were swindling you cos they might get all the money from the shares or whatever they put it in."

"Well the banks take your money and they say to other people 'do you want to borrow it' and then they get interest which they share out with people who save money with them."

Some children saw interest as a kind of free gift: "It's just an offer, to get you encouraged, to get you to use the bank."

This understanding of interest rates is a further development of the institutionalisation of saving noted in the 9 year olds. Just as for that age group, to save means to use the bank, but now it means to use the bank to get interest.

Saving as a Temptation Inhibiting Strategy. Most of the boys at this age recognised that temptation to spend their money was a real problem and that banks were a solution to this problem. After interest rates this was the most often mentioned feature of banks.

E: So you put your money in the bank for the interest?
C: Yea, and so I don't spend it as well. . .if it was left over I wouldn't have any cos I would always be at the pictures or swimming or something.

So the illiquidity of saved money was a very positive aspect of banks;

E: Do you think a bank helps you to save?
C: Yes, cos you can never get in to take your money out.
E: Is that why you put your money in?
C: Yes, cos it stops me from spending it.

The Role of Parents in Saving. Along with a growing awareness of the institutional nature of saving there is an increasing recognition of the role parents play in children's economic affairs and the need to negotiate with them. Most bank accounts are outside the control of children themselves and most of the savings made are not voluntary (although the children may agree with it) and are not in fact made by the children. Parents act to instil good saving habits: "I get £5 a month from my mum cos if I got say a bit each week, I'd just spend it all. This way I have to save over the month to have some money" and this aim is explicitly recognised by some of the boys:

E: Is there anything else you can think of that makes it a worthwhile idea to save?
C: Well, Mum's always telling me that I've got something then if I want to buy a car or rent a car or a flat.

There are also more "moral" constructions of the importance of saving:

"I put money away like I said, every week or so, so I can use it to go out to places instead of asking my mum, cos I don't like asking my mum for money cos it makes me feel guilty after, I know that's wrong, but I can't rely on her all the time, so I better learn to use my own money."

Here we can see the child's saving bound up with his relationships and the anticipation of future independence.

DISCUSSION OF STUDY 4

The socio-developmental approach, introduced in Chapter 1, is based on the idea that childrens' economic actions are functional expressions, often through formal or institutional means, of socially determined ideas of acceptable economic goals, and that saving is a functional response to the demands of the all-pervading income constraint. In Chapter 3 we went on to study the way in which children at different ages solved the problems that such constraints present. In particular we looked at children's understanding of the inclusive relationship between present and future purchases, and the management of finances by saving when under threat either from external (a robber) or internal sources (desires for immediate gratification). The results from these studies helped us identify two general developmental trends. First, a move from a non-functional to a functional understanding of saving, and second (and relatedly) a move from defining them in social terms to defining them in economic terms. Young children put their money in the bank because it was a "good" thing to do in social terms, although on many occasions these responses were inappropriate in functional terms. Older children saved because it was a good thing to do in economic terms; it served a specific economic function. This move towards an economic understanding of the basis of value was most clearly shown in Study 3. Young children were prepared to lose money going across a toll bridge rather than being robbed by a "naughty robber". Similarly the value of saving, as just mentioned, was seen in purely social terms by young children and in economic terms by older children.

In the present experiment we set out to see how closely the changes catalogued in Studies 1, 2 and 3 would mirror money management under income constraint in a more free ranging naturalistic situation. As we see it, the board game approach could be inadequate in two vital ways. The first is centred around the issue of relevance. Do income constraints present the same sorts of problems for children as they do for adults? If the answer to this question is no, then the whole idea of the board game studies was ill-conceived. The second concerns the accuracy of the characterisation of the development of functional saving made possible by these controlled and highly structured studies. Did the structure of the game constrain the child's expression of a functional approach to saving or, on the other hand, influence the frequency of saving responses made? Were the developmental trends identified a real reflection of changes in actual conceptions of economic activity or simply artifacts of the board game situation?

The Relevance of Income Constraints

Although the need to situate saving explicitly within its social and cultural context was seen as the basis for our functional understanding of economic action, we have paid little attention to this issue so far in the book. As we see it, this social context plays two quite distinct roles in defining what constitutes effective economic activity during childhood. First, as we have already mentioned, it provides information about acceptable economic goals and behaviours. In Chapter 5 we will have a closer look at the types of representations of acceptable economic aspirations available to the child. Second, the social and economic support provided through close personal relationships may actually modify the types of demands imposed on the child by apparent economic constraint. In particular the generosity of parents might mean that children do not face real constraints on income.

Certainly some of the children in the present study expected their parents (and the experimenter) to "top up" their savings. But there is little doubt that even the most doting parents will not continuously give in to the promptings of their child. But this study does suggest that although the constraint is real, saving is just one way in which children solve the economic problems presented by it; they can deal with some problems by simply getting more money, either through manipulating their parents or by earning it. So a child who wants to buy a canoe may "save up" his pocket money, but it is just as likely that he will ask for it as a Christmas present or make a deal with his parents that if he saves half, they will pay the other half.

What this study does show quite clearly is that children's saving cannot be divorced from the family environment or the wider social context. In the family the power relationship between parent and child and parental aims for their child's economic behaviour will be significant; the family's position in society will also be important. This is particularly true of parents who themselves are living on a small budget. While the children who took part in the present study were mostly from secure middle class backgrounds, obviously there are many parents, let alone children, who live in relative poverty. The development of the economic competence of their children may of course proceed along a very different course. A recent conversation I had with a 9 year old girl living the East End of London, whose mother was an unemployed single parent bears this out. When I asked her why she saved the money given to her by her Grandma, she replied that she saved to help mummy out with the bills. One would expect that this sort of financial pressure would certainly concentrate the mind of the child and influence the course of her developing understandings of economic aspects of everyday life.

In summary then, it is quite clear that income constraints do present real problems for children and so the board game studies presented in Chapter 3 set the children a problem that they would be familiar with.

The Generalisability of Developmental Trends
Isolated During the Board Game Studies

Although the children taking part in Experiments 1, 2 and 3 were tackling problems that they would be familiar with in their everyday life, we still face the problem that the trends in the way that problems were understood and dealt with might not give a true reflection of development in the "real world". Although the present study was also a relatively artificial situation it certainly gave greater scope for the child to map real world constructions of economic actions onto their "play" equivalents than did the board game studies.

Similar trends *were* identified in the behaviour of the children in the two situations. First, both approaches demonstrate that between the ages of 6 and 12 our children's ability to save improves. In both types of situations this was associated with an increasingly functional understanding of saving. In the present study this was shown by an increasingly sophisticated understanding of the role of saving as a means of ensuring safety for money as well as the increasing use of the bank as part of the relatively sophisticated economic strategies.

The trend for the value of actions to be increasingly defined in economic as opposed to social terms is also supported by this study. For instance, young children explained interest as money that the bank has saved and uses to reward good behaviour, whereas older children saw it as payment for money loaned. The present study does cast doubt on the findings of the board game studies in one important respect. In Study 1 we suggested that the fact that young children defined the value of economic actions in social terms led to a contradiction between their views that money saved was money lost and that saving was a socially desirable thing to do. This contradiction seems to have been resolved by a high level of non-functional and (in the eyes of the child) expensive saving. In the present study although this tension was still apparent it was not resolved in the same way. The 6 year old children in this study did certainly not engage in the same levels of saving as their counterparts in the previous studies. One possible explanation for this is that the highly structured series of opportunities to visit the banks in the board game studies, and the questioning of the experimenter, enhanced the social desirability of saving. It is possible then that the board games over-emphasised young children's interest in saving. This age group don't actually seem to like saving very much at all. By contrast the older children are quite keen on saving particularly because it gives a return in the form of interest.

Institutionalised Saving and the Role of Interest

One of the aims of this study was to disambiguate the relationship between money box saving and institutionalised saving. Our earlier study used a set of money boxes to represent a bank, and we argued earlier that this was a problem and attempted to set up a more reasonable and realistic bank in this play economy. The function of this bank was to allow institutionalised saving to be available as a strategy in the game and to make explicit the distinction between banks and money boxes.

Unfortunately, the bank was the weakest part of the set-up. It was important that the bank be integrated into the game in a functional way (so that all the children could, if they wished, use the bank as a saving strategy) and that it was conceptually distinct from the money box. For the latter to be the case, the money box itself needed to fulfil a saving function, which in practice it did not. The money box was used primarily as a convenient receptacle for carrying tokens around—a kind of large plastic purse. The comparatively short time the game took (two hours maximum) meant that it was not sensible to perceive the money box as a saving aid, although they are used as such in the home, whereas the bank did appear real to the children and was a helpful saving device. The bank, however, was not without its problems. The actual functioning of the bank (that is, that money could both be deposited and withdrawn) was not made explicit to all subjects, which may have led some children (particularly the 6 year olds) not to use the bank at all. In addition, the actual initial transaction at the bank (which involved tokens being represented in a bank book) was not understood by all the children. However, these are not intractable problems. If more care were taken to set up a more detailed mock bank, with perhaps a second experimenter as a bank assistant, the role and reality of the bank could be more easily established. Similarly, since most children had bank books of some kind, if those used in the game were more professional with more time being taken over the transaction, the difficulty of understanding notional money could easily be overcome. Despite these problems, the interview material gathered in the bank environment was very rich.

5

Social Influences on Children's Saving

INTRODUCTION

In Chapter 1 we outlined an alternative approach to the study of the development of economic thought and action during childhood. At the heart of this approach was the recognition of the role played by social representations of legitimate goals of economic behaviour in setting up both the types of economic problems faced, and defining the legitimacy of the solutions given, by the children in Western industrial cultures. By doing this we highlighted the functional significance of children's economic behaviour. In Chapters 3 and 4 we concentrated on the role of one particular set of actions—saving—in providing the solution to one type of economic problem that was posed by the existence of an income constraint. In this chapter we will try to gain some idea of the type of representations of saving presented to children by two very influential agents: the parents of the children and those responsible for marketing the services of the savings institutions. By doing this we will also attempt to piece together the types of lay theories of the development of saving held by these two groups.

THE DEVELOPMENT OF ECONOMIC IDEALS WITHIN POPULAR CULTURE

It is clear that children come into contact with the common language of our populist economic culture in a variety of ways. They listen to adult conversation, they are given advice, they see advertisements and so on. One might expect that to a large extent this language and the accompanying images would colour the ways in which these children understand their own economic behaviour, its value and functions. This would mean that those who have control over this language play an important role in determining these attitudes.

Often in modern society these sources of influence are found to originate from those who have a vested interest in encouraging certain actions. The government may encourage saving to combat rising inflation or encourage spending when a country's economy is depressed. When it comes to children's saving there are two real sources of influence. First there are those who are responsible for marketing the services of the saving institutions. It is clear that these agents have a vested interest in encouraging both a general commitment from children to save and a specific interest in promoting their own institution as the best place to save. Second, there are the children's parents. One would expect parents to have a rather different and perhaps more benign interest, with their prime concern being to teach their children to provide for the future by saving.

The first stage in satisfying these different interests is for both these groups of people to develop a theory of the best way to teach children to save—what type of language should they use? What type of saving regime should be encouraged? Should they explain to children the functions of saving or simply reward good saving practice? In order to try to understand the way that the act of saving is represented to children we will look first at the nature of social representations of economic action in general and saving in particular, both as they exist today and briefly, as in the recent history of Western societies. This will lead on to some empirical studies of the types of theories upon which parents and marketeers base their attempts to encourage children to save.

REPRESENTATIONS OF ECONOMIC ACTIONS; SOME GENERAL CONSIDERATIONS

Available representations of economic actions may contain three different types of information. The first two involve the presentation of information about the value of certain economic actions. On the one hand there are those that prescribe a certain attitude to an economic act. These are based on a categorical definition of value. For instance, we might be told that "it is bad to borrow money . . .". On the other, there are those representations that describe the purpose of an action and so emphasise the functional basis of economic action; ". . . but you can provide capital for home improvements by borrowing money . . .". The third type of information is simply descriptive, giving information about aspects of the system of institutions, such as banks, that aid economic practice; ". . . and we can lend you money at a reasonable rate of interest".

If we look at these distinctions in terms of children's saving, we see that advertisers might choose to adopt language that emphasises a categorical view of the value of saving and prescribes a certain view of the value of thrift. They might emphasise a functional view and describe the importance of providing for a rainy day. Finally they might simply rely on reporting a change in their own rate of interest. Of course along with this type of information may come an implicit view of saving as an investment.

THE HISTORICAL CONTEXT

In general historical terms one particular metaphor has underpinned our Western conception of economic actions; that of "economic man". The most common characterisation is of a person who; "behaves within the limits of his freedom . . . so as to maximize something good" (Rachlin, 1980, p.206).

McCloskey (1986, p.24) put this in more emotive terms when he wrote; "the history of all hitherto existing societies is the history of interactions among selfish individuals".

Whereas economists have tended to see this view of the economic man in the abstract, others have adopted a different view. For economists it is one of the axioms upon which modern(ist) economic analysis is based. These axioms are formal statements about how individuals will behave given certain choices. They are simply thought to be powerful simplifications of human motivation. They are used in order to study the large and complex system that is a modern economy. Their validity is not an empirical matter (Simmons, 1974). As Lea, Tarpy, and Webley write (1987, p.108): "Economic man is a distinct species from homo sapiens. Real people are not expected to obey the theory."

Indeed Friedman (1953) has argued that whether or not the views expressed have any "truth", behaviourally or morally, is unimportant so long as the predictions about aggregate economic behaviour that they allow economists to make are meaningful and on the whole correct.

The idea that this view of "rational" action functions other than in this way has a number of proponents. They argue that it serves more as an expression of the legitimacy of economic practices presently dominant in Western industrial societies than as a formal set of axioms. According to Abercrombie, Hill & Turner (1986) the concept of economic man prescribes a set of desires and intentions underpinning the pursuit of individual well-being that are synonymous with the economic actions of citizenship in these cultures. From this perspective it would be claimed that our understanding of our own economic practice has been determined by a representation of the acquisition of individual wealth in the pursuit of personal well-being, this in turn being the product of the historical process of individualisation, which many economic historians and sociologists believe started in Europe during the reformation and renaissance (Fullerton, 1928; Robertson, 1933; Weber, 1904).

This type of analysis is given a more developmental flavour by Kessen (1979) who in his essay *The child and other cultural inventions*, has argued that developmental psychologists need to reject the notion of a singular child, and in so doing recognise the role that cultural and historical processes play in the construction of that child. Thus the idea of rationality encapsulated in the "economic man" metaphor is but one cultural expression of human motives, to which the child becomes socialised, and which is at the same time reproduced within that child. On one level then, individual economic development is a process of the reproduction of culturally derived representations of legitimate action—specifically the desire to maximise individual well-being. The history of the development of economic institutions and agencies in Western culture has involved the provision of increasingly efficient means to this broadly defined end. It is only when one places the modern economic world in its historical context that the function of economic action, the role of economic institutions and so the meaning and significance of developments in children's economic thought and action become clear.

Historically, at least, calls to saving have emphasised the categorical definition of value so that the topic of saving has been the subject of a specific set of representations. In this case the representation about the value and legitimacy of economic goals are coloured by what Lea et al. (1987) have called the "pseudo-morality" of thrift.

Traditionally, this quality of character has been seen as a virtue in many societies. La Fontaine (1668–1679/1974) put Aesop's fable about the ant and the grasshopper first in his collection. Samuel Smiles (1875) dedicated an entire book to discussing thrift and its virtues. Keynes (1936) reports that de Mandeville's fable of the bees (which argues that thrift is evil) was so badly received that it was judged to be nuisance by a grand jury in Middlesex in 1723.

THE MARKETEERS' VIEW OF SAVING

But what role does this emphasis on saving as being of value in itself play in modern day economic rhetoric? To answer this we have analysed the types of theories of saving motives implicit in the language of the marketing strategies produced by the major savings institutions to encourage both adults and children to save.

In Studies 5 and 6 we compared the information contained in the savings advertisements designed to encourage saving by adults and children in order to examine the institutions' theories of the development and maintenance of saving in these two groups. Clearly the relevance of theories of why people save is limited by the aims of the marketing people. In terms of the adult market, those responsible for marketing savings accounts are concerned with two problems: how to get people to save more, and how to get people to save with them. The received wisdom among the advertising fraternity (at least, that publicly presented when they wish to minimise their role, as in the cigarette advertising debate) is that only the second is of any significance. In this case we would expect their marketing strategy to reflect only theories about why people switch accounts rather than why they save in the first place. But we do not need to take advertisers at their word. The evidence suggests that advertising can increase demand for a product class. McGuiness and Cowling (1975) for instance, showed that advertising did increase the aggregate demand for cigarettes in the UK in the 1960s. Presumably, advertisers are as aware of this as anyone.

The approach taken here was to examine two classes of advertising material to discover what theories they embodied, what metaphors were employed and how saving and its' alternatives were portrayed.

STUDY 5: ENCOURAGING ADULT SAVING

The Sample of Material

The material sampled included all the building society advertisements appearing in *The Times*, the *Guardian*, the *Daily Telegraph* and their associated Sunday papers during February, 1985. Duplicates were ignored. This left 61 unique adverts from 37 separate building societies. Clearly, a more direct examination of marketeers' theories could be obtained by interviews, since the published adverts are probably a compromise between clients' views, the advertising agencies' views and what is legally permitted. But the published material presented in Studies 5 and 6 is a reasonable proxy measure and has the advantage that it is not distorted by an interviewee's desire to put a good face on their behaviour.

The Analysis

The emphasis here is on the content of adverts, and what the content tells us about the theories of saving held by the marketing fraternity. We have made no attempt to analyse the data quantitatively, not because such an analysis is impossible, but because we believe that traditional quantitative content analysis would, in this instance, give a spurious air of objectivity. To enable the reader to assess the adequacy of our interpretations we have reproduced as many examples as possible.

RESULTS

Interest Rates

The most striking feature of the adverts is the emphasis they place on the interest rate of the account. Even if those adverts that are little more than announcements of rate changes are excluded, interest rates still dominate. The best example of this is an advert for the Leicester Building Society, which takes up two half pages and states baldly in letters 27cm high "8.75% +". In much smaller letters is the slogan "You only get the extra if you move to the Leicester", from which it seems a reasonable deduction that interest rates are seen as crucial to the switching between accounts. A similar theme is evident in the Birmingham and Bridgewater's "Definitely first rate" and Skipton's "9.7% net. THE BEST ON THE MARKET". That most of this kind of advertising is comparative is clear and a particularly good exemplar is the Chelsea: "10.80% The Chelsea Capital Shares Challenge. Any building society . . . that can match this interest . . . should speak up now . . . . . . Hmmm. Quiet isn't it."

Other Characteristics of Accounts

The other main feature of the adverts was that they emphasised relevant features of the accounts, such as liquidity, guaranteed rate differentials and cheque book facilities. The Coventry 3-year bond is a good example, stressing that "11.10% means 2.85% guaranteed extra interest" and ramming home the message with the comment that "interest rates can go up or down. But our new 3-year bond gives you a full 2.85% extra interest . . . guaranteed for 3 years". Skipton highlights the instant access to its Sovereign account: "Skipton pays a better rate . . . and no strings".

Names, Metaphors and Slogans

The names of many of the accounts conjure up the image of intrinsic, indestructible value. There are "Cheltenham Gold", "Silver link", "Bullion shares", "Diamond shares" and perhaps the cleverest, since it conveys in addition ease of access, "Liquid Gold". Others reiterate the importance of their purported higher rates of interest, for example: "90 day Xtra", "Money Spinner Plus".

Perhaps more interesting are the metaphors lurking in the graphics. We find the idea of security (the pyramid of Anglia); saving for a rainy day (clouds and rainbow of the Derbyshire, with the associated slogan, "forecasting a brighter future"); risk, in competitor's accounts naturally (a mousetrap, and the slogan, "with triple bonus you can still earn 10.3% without getting caught"); and yet again interest rate (the Abbey National's gondola, and the slogan "come on up to the Abbey National's new seven day level").

COMMENT

There is surprisingly little variety in these adverts. Consequently there appears to be considerable consensus among those responsible as to what people are looking for in building society accounts. They clearly see possible consumers as rational individuals making informed choice between their own account and those of their competitors. More specifically they seem to hold a Katona (1975) type model of saving; that savings are a consumer good like any other. Following Lancaster (1966), we know that goods have a variety of important characteristics and that people try to buy those goods that combine the characteristics they want with a good price. It is obvious that those marketing saving accounts believe this; hence the emphasis on rates of interest, instant access, cheque books and so on, and the associated names and slogans. They emphasised neither a functional or categorical definition of value. Consequently there were few attempts to explain general reasons for saving (security in old age, rainy day saving) and in general the moral tone of historical calls to saving was absent. However a particularly striking example of this approach can be seen in the images used in a National Westminster Bank advert featuring a man holding a cheque with two figures either side of his head; a devil urging him to spend it and an angel urging him to save it (the resolution of this problem is to "do both, with our monthly income account").

All this suggests that the advertisers were indeed not interested in encouraging saving in general. Rather these adverts overwhelmingly reflected a concern with the problem of "how to get people to save with them". Implicit in this approach is the belief that adults are well aware both of the value of saving and its functions; what they need is information about what is the best or most profitable way of saving.

STUDY 6: ENCOURAGING CHILDREN'S SAVING

With children it might be expected that the aims of the savings institutions would be quite different. They have both to teach children to save and to persuade them to do it with them. We have drawn a distinction between theories that stress the functional value of saving, such as Freidman's, and those that emphasise the categorical view of saving; that saving is of value in and of itself—either because it provides wealth that is of value itself or because it represents an expression of thrift. In Chapters 3 and 4, we drew a distinction between children's functional and non-functional understandings of saving at different ages and the role these might play in the development of effective saving. Consequently it is important to look at whether the theories used by the savings institutions that colour their calls for children to save emphasise either of these aspects of saving.

The Material Sampled

The body of material collected was that aimed at young savers by the banks and the building societies. Children's accounts were opened at the four main banks, and the publicity material and associated promotional material scrutinised. In addition, leaflets on special children's accounts were obtained from 11 building societies. Because the banks have in the past paid interest gross and building societies have paid it net, the latter have not competed for children's savings by setting up special accounts. A very few societies do offer something special, but only the Woolwich comes close to the generous offerings of the banks. So here we concentrate on the special bank accounts. Each will be dealt with in turn.

RESULTS

Barclays: This bank discriminated on the grounds of the child's age. For under 7s, a folder, pen, ruler etc; for over 7s, a magazine ("packed with articles, money making ideas . . .") and a money box. In the associated booklet *How to make your money grow*, the child is told that "A Supersaver account is a simple way to start saving. And a great way to make money, too". Interest is defined as "the money we pay you for saving with us and letting us use your money". One interesting feature is that if a supersaver recruits another child, £1 is credited to the recruiter's account.

Lloyds: They operated a Black Horse young savers account, which comes along with a money box and a folder. The message to the young saver mentions only one function of the account, that of saving up for something special. Interest is referred to but not defined, since it is clearly assumed that children (or at least super-savers) know what it is.

Midland: The listening bank has a Griffin Savers Account which offers extra interest and an extensive savers kit (a sports bag, geometry set, action file, dictionary, badge and a magazine). It seems to be aimed at older children and apart from the goodies and the magazine (which has no items specifically on saving) is very similar to an adult account. One interesting comment is that they require a minimum of £10 in the account "for at least 6 months to encourage a saving *habit*" (our emphasis).

National Westminster: They have put together the most sophisticated package; a savings scheme for children rather than just a savings account. As their leaflet says: "All too often, younger children regard saving as a dull and disappointing alternative to spending . . . Young NatWest Piggy Bankers are encouraged to save by a sequence of rewards, in the form of beautifully crafted ceramic piggy banks". These are sent to the child as the account passes set thresholds (£25, £50, £75, and £100). The child is also given "Woody's wobbly money tree"; a wall chart depicting a pile of 50p coins that can be coloured in. There is also *Piggy Press*, a regular newsletter.

Woolwich Building Society: They offer a stamp album, a packet of stamps and a magazine, and the account is clearly aimed at younger children, featuring, as it does, Henry's cat. This cartoon animal introduces the account with an 800 word story, which pits the virtues of money boxes (not NatWest Piggies) against having an account with the Woolwich. As Henry says "the money is safe . . . and what is more they pay me to save with them". "That sounds interesting" says Mosey Mouse; "It is interesting, in fact it is interest and that is what they call it. When you leave your money in for a while it grows larger so you get out more than you put in. That extra amount is called 'interest'." replies Henry's cat.

Bristol and West: They operate a stamp saving scheme featuring Snoopy and the child gets a badge for joining. They stress saving up for something special by saving a bit now and again and explain interest as "a sort of reward—it's the money we pay you for lending us your savings".

Halifax: The world's largest building society has a special club for young people—the Little Xtra Club. The membership pack contains a money box house, a bike sticker, a badge and a club magazine. The aim is "to make saving fun" and explicitly to foster the "learning [of] an important lesson which will be of value for the rest of . . . life". Saving up is stressed.

Anglia: They have a Top Saver Club for the under 18s. When you join, you get a blue wallet with a notepad, pen and target savings chart and a magazine. More imaginatively, the novice Top Saver receives a "Start Collecting" gift as an introduction to a new hobby (e.g. coins, wildlife cards). Every time £5 is added to the account, the holder gets more items to add to their collection. What is more there is a birthday bonus, described as "your special reward for saving".

Cheltenham & Gloucester: The Cheltenham & Gloucester rely on the charms of Paddington to sell their Junior account, which is in fact identical to their investment share account for adults. *Paddington opens a saving account*, a story involving the ubiquitous marmalade sandwiches, explains what is involved. The two features of note are that interest is described as "a thank you from the C & G", (the C & G "give you a present of some extra money") and that, yet again, saving up for special things is cited as the reason for saving.

Other building societies: Many only offer the normal share account, operated by a parent, some offer badges, balloons, magazines etc. but these are not serious marketing efforts.

COMMENT

In this material there is very little emphasis on teaching children the functional aspects of the value of saving. Although three campaigns (Lloyds, Bristol & West, and Cheltenham & Gloucester) did introduce the notion of saving up for something special, the main emphasis was on non-functional aspects of saving. This involved either presenting saving as a "good" habit that can be rewarded either explicitly by providing extra incentives (as with NatWest Piggies, and the Anglia's collecting scheme and birthday bonus) or implicitly through the addition of the "prize" for saving; interest to the money deposited. This presentation of interest as a prize or reward is interesting given what we already know about what children think interest is. For instance we know from the work of Jahoda (1984) that one third of a group of Glaswegian 11 year olds had no knowledge of interest. Very few had any idea of the connection between lending, borrowing, and interest. Our own 12 year old boys in Study 4 did seem to have a clearer grasp of the economic basis of interest. But, all in all, banks have probably adopted the right approach to explaining interest by using simple metaphors and symbols. Anglia Building Society adopted a slightly different approach, making the connection between collecting and saving. This could be construed merely as a reward but there are of course Freudian connotations. All the institutions want to make saving "fun" and provide extra incentives (the goodies) to encourage children to save with them. But compared to the adverts, in this material we see more general models of how to influence children to save more, and no explicit comparisons with other possible homes for their savings.

What is clear is that there is very little attempt to present any explicit view of either the functional or categorical value of saving. It appears that the marketeers believe that saving is seen as a response like any other, the probability of which can best be increased by rewards rather than descriptions of its functions or the rhetoric of thrift. But this emphasis on the reinforcement of saving behaviour may have implicit connotations for the child's understanding of the value of saving. That is to say that any explicit emphasis on the moral dimension to saving is conspicuous by its absence, although the rewards schedules arranged by the banks may provide implicit information about the value of saving. This position would certainly seem to explain Hussein's (1981) findings. She looked at how children handled money and found that: "if they were to be believed these children simply handled their pocket money for the brief space of time it took to put it in a money box . . . the giving of money is, in these cases little more than a ritualised lesson in saving, an activity which it was clear from the tone of the answers was held in high esteem" (p.21).

Whether savings institutions believe that reference to specific aspects of the "moral" worth of saving would be ineffective, or they simply feel that they are not in a position to use such value-laden language is unclear.

In Studies 5 and 6 we have looked at the representations of saving implicit in savings advertisements and schemes in order to get an idea of the lay theories of saving held by marketeers. We can see that the theories implicit in the language and images used are highly dependent on the aims of the marketeers. They are interested in persuading adults to switch accounts and children to develop a saving habit.

The strategies adopted to achieve these two ends have one thing in common. On the whole, marketing aimed at both adults and children spends very little time discussing the functions of saving in general. Although a more intimate study of attitudes might be helpful, it appears that the marketeers assume that adults already understand the benefits of various functions of saving, and with children they appear to believe that outlining the values of saving will not influence their saving behaviour.

But the main point of interest is that they appear to make no attempt to encourage an understanding of the role of saving in effective budgeting; an understanding that these institutions seem to assume already exists in adults. So how then is this functional understanding of saving acquired?

PARENTS' INFLUENCE ON CHILDREN'S SAVING

In Chapter 4 we demonstrated how the development of children's saving is intimately tied up with the power relationships between parents and children. This combined with the parents desire to influence their children's present behaviour and so ensure their future security might play a significant role in the development of effective saving. In Study 7 we will examine the different types of approaches taken by parents to children's saving. In Studies 5 and 6 we looked at the approach taken by savings institutions to encourage children's saving. Such vested interests determine children's understandings of saving because to some extent they control the types of images of saving available to children. Although parents have this type of control as well, they also have the financial power to exert a more direct type of control, which follows from their children's financial dependence.

Clearly, this dependence could prove important in the process of socialisation of economic attitudes and the development of economic practices during childhood. This means that parents can influence their children's understandings of the economic world in a much more direct way than the advertising agents or marketeers. For instance, this might be achieved by parental teachings about the value of saving and the role of saving in effective money management. These would be made more salient if made during a visit to a bank to deposit some money in an account. On the other hand, parents, like the savings institutions, might simply attempt to encourage a savings habit either by forcing or rewarding a certain level of saving. In the last part of this chapter on the social context of saving we will look at the ways in which parents use their power to reward certain views of the value of saving and other economic practices.

The approach adopted was different from those used in previous studies looking at the relationship between children's saving and parents' attitudes (Marshall & Magruder, 1960). We used open-ended interviews with parents to provide a series of accounts of such things as the role of pocket money, the value of saving and the need to provide for their child's future. Clearly this type of approach is not intended to give an exhaustive account of parents' views of saving but rather to constitute an attempt to look at some of the possible roles that parents play in the development of their children's understanding and practice of saving.

STUDY 7: PARENTS' VIEWS OF CHILDREN'S SAVING

Most of the parents of the thirty 6, 9 and 12 year old boys who had taken part in the play economy described in Chapter 4 were contacted and asked if they would be willing to be interviewed about their children's saving and related topics. Parents were interviewed in their own homes. Sometimes both parents were interviewed together; sometimes only one parent was available for interview or they were interviewed separately. The interview was open ended and centred around four main topics: (1) pocket money: if it was given, reasons for this, the age at which it was first given (or would be given) and general information about the pocket money set-up; (2) accounts: if the child had a bank, building society or post office account and follow-up questions looking at when and by whom the accounts were opened, access to the accounts and anecdotes about the use of accounts; (3) children's own sources of income: what they were (e.g. birthday money) and their status, control and use; (4) parents own saving history—what parents did as children. Each interview lasted approximately 30–45 minutes. They were transcribed and the transcripts analysed by comparing and contrasting the answers given by parents. Both consistency and inconsistency was sought in the discourse and a general picture obtained. Anecdotal material was treated as a useful source of information. The content of these interviews will be discussed under a number of different headings.

RESULTS

Parents' Views of the Value of Saving

The reason for the savings institutions' attempts to try to encourage children to save was quite easy to discern: profit. But why should we expect parents to be concerned with their children's saving?

It is certainly considered appropriate by most people for parents to have a healthy concern for the long term well-being of their children. It would be considered unusual for a parent not to try to ensure that their children have a comfortable life when they grow up. When the transcripts of the interviews were analysed it became quite clear that most parents shared this concern for their children's future. But of course this need not necessarily lead the parents to encourage their children to save for themselves. The most straightforward way of dealing with this need not involve their children at all. Parents can provide for their children's future by simply opening a savings account on their behalf. The child need not know of the account's existence and may be pleasantly surprised when told about it when older. The process of depositing money need not involve the child and the account need not even have been opened under the child's name. While this approach would certainly leave children wealthier it would be unlikely to leave them wiser.

The child would not have been told about the benefits of saving or been given practical information about how to save, or even been given basic practice in the act of depositing money at the bank. This approach to providing for the child's future would serve no educational purpose at all. As a consequence it might be expected that the children of parents who adopted this approach to providing for the future would spend the money as soon as it was under their control. In this situation the prudence of parents would be no guard against a spendthrift child.

Parental Control of Children's Economic Affairs

From the interviews we could see that parents held a wide range of beliefs about the extent to which they considered themselves responsible for encouraging individual responsibility in financial affairs. The parents who did feel that their responsibility extended much further than simply hoarding money adopted a number of different approaches to this task. In the following section we have tried to characterise the different approaches taken by parents in terms of the extent to which the child was given access to money and the extent to which the parents had control over what that money was used for. As you will see these approaches ranged from parents making no attempt to constrain the amount of pocket money that was spent, to those where children were given no control at all over what they bought.

Personal Saving and Pocket Money

Pocket Money as Spending Money.   On the level of practical experience of saving, one would imagine that pocket money provides the perfect vehicle for the type of practice needed of making decisions in favour of the future and so experiencing the benefits of that activity. Given this, one might expect that the giving of pocket money might be accompanied by a message about the value of saving and even some guidelines about the amount of money that ought to be spent and the amount that ought to be saved. But for many parents pocket money is not seen as a vehicle for teaching about saving.

On the contrary the pocket money given by a large majority of parents was designed as spending money. Encouraging saving was not the prime motive of the parents and money was given free of obligations. Parents did not mind if the money was spent; clearly pocket money was not used as a means to educate the child about the virtues of saving. That pocket money was "free" money can be seen in the replies to the question "why did you decide to give your child pocket money?". The replies centred around the need to make money available to the children to buy sweets etc.—rather than in terms of the need to teach children the value of money or how to save. This is not to say that the answers given exclude the possibility of these other factors playing some part in the reasoning behind the giving of pocket money on some levels, but the first response was in terms of spending rather than saving.

> MRS. B: "I suppose because at that age they could just about go down the local shop and buy a handful of sweets or a toy aeroplane or something. Yes it was because of that. I can't think of any other reason."

MRS. G: "So that they don't keep asking me for money. It's so they can go and buy their sweets or their birthday presents or whatever."

Interestingly whether or not pocket money was given did not depend on the parents' estimations of their children's aptitude for dealing with abstract concepts like money, or their perceived readiness to learn about saving. Rather these decisions were made on the basis of practical considerations, e.g. whether the child was able to spend the money.

Q: "How come you started giving them pocket money?"
MR. S: "I've always done, well, since they were 4 or 5. It's useless giving them before that because they've really nothing to spend it on anyway. But when they come of age, when there is something they really want to buy themselves, well . . ."

If parents do take advantage of the opportunity for learning provided by pocket money, it is in the area of spending rather than the more difficult and restrictive area of saving.

MRS. S: "First it was mainly for sweeties, to get them used to going down and asking for sweets themselves and giving the money and getting the change."

Pocket money is an integral part of teaching children about economic exchange for some parents. For these parents, ideas of children's saving pocket money are only understood in this context.

An extension of this "pocket money as spending money" scenario can be seen in some aspects of some parents' child management strategies. For instance, pocket money becomes a way to diffuse previously fraught situations where money was an issue, and serves to facilitate smoother running of parent/offspring relations:

Q: "Besides stopping the argument about how much they were going to get, was there any other motivation behind starting a system like this?"
MS. F: "Peace for me, I think! It's just a way of organising things I think. If you've got three children there is always lots and lots of areas of dispute you know . . . and it's just, I try to reduce the areas of dispute. They know what they can expect from me—and it just keeps things on an even keel a bit more, I think."

Parents are actually quite explicit about the lack of any guidelines for the uses to which the pocket money should be put:

MR. W: "I mean, I pay for nearly everything they have . . . It's just a treat really, for something they want for themselves."
Q: "So that pound they get for pocket money, that's designed to be spent?"

MRS. P: "If they want to yes. It's up to them what they do with it."
MR. P: "To be squandered to a certain extent."

While this general approach to pocket money was very common it could be said to mark the most casual approach of parents to their child's economic education. It is important to recognise that all of the parents who gave pocket money without strings had a much stricter approach to institutionalised saving. As we will see later not one of the parents interviewed suggested that their children would be given (easy) access to bank or building society accounts or control over what the money in those accounts should be spent on.

Saving Half: Parents Attempts to Direct Saving.   It needs to be restated here that children are (with one exception in this sample) wholly dependent on their parents in terms of finance. They have no independent means of income and invariably no independent control over the larger sums of money that are held in accounts in their name. Thus pocket money is the only way children can have control over money. As has been stated earlier, the small amount of money provided by parents is given without any obligations; they can spend it or save it as they wish.

Thus, if the child wishes to buy an item that costs more than the weekly pocket money sum, the child needs to engage in spontaneous saving of this "free" source of money. At least as far as the parents interviewed for this study are aware, this type of spontaneous saving is a rather uncommon phenomenon. But children can of course employ a different strategy to attempt to increase their disposable wealth. These other strategies can involve either a direct appeal to the parents for the item, or aided saving. This form of saving involves negotiations between parents and children. In Chapter 4 we reported that many children in the study expected their parents (and the experimenter in some instances) to help them out by contributing money if they wanted to buy an expensive item. This was often agreed as long as they made some attempt to save up for that item first. The children's accounts are corroborated by the parents' accounts:

MR. M: ". . . they see something in the shop they like, which costs a lot and, well, we simply say . . . we either buy it for them, for their birthday or Christmas or something, or we say, look you save up . . . and if its pretty expensive, say more than £10 or something we will say 'look, you save half of it and we'll put the other half towards it,' but they rarely do save."

As can be seen, saving up half is offered by some parents as a strategy for increasing spending power. Saving up half of £10 with an average income of £1 a week is a long term commitment. It appears from parents' reports that this strategy, although often available to the child, is rarely taken up:

MRS. P: "I don't think he's ever saved the whole sum for anything, has he"
MR. P: "I think he's put two weeks together with his money, but it doesn't go very far. It's a long way for a child isn't it really."

It appears then as if this "saving half" strategy is rarely a viable or successful option for the child (at least for these pre-adolescents) though simply showing willing may achieve very little:

MR. P: "As long as they show initiative, I don't mind chucking a bit more in, but I'm not going to put money after money, y'know, giving pocket money and then buying things as well. He's never gone without really, I mean toys and that, if they are reasonable I mean I won't buy things I don't think are worth the money."

With this saving half strategy parents are attempting to give their children some kind of functional understanding of the role of saving, at the same time rewarding their attempts to save by contributing extra money. This means essentially that the role of parents in this situation is to encourage saving either by reward or by verbal encouragement. In addition the parents are also giving the child implicit information about the value of saving as a means of buying birthday presents and other large items.

Enforced Saving of Money that is not Spent. A third approach to encouraging children's saving of disposable income was suggested by another of the mothers:

MRS. O: "M. has money in his hand everyday to go to school. He has a pound to get him to school and back and he comes home and gives me the change, the first thing he does is give me the change . . . And if we're out and they want a couple of marbles from the marble shop, I'll say, you've got 50p each to buy marbles, and that somehow feels nicer than giving them money at random—they handle that a lot better."

Here the mother saves the money for the child. The practice of giving the change from the journey to school is enforced. In this case though the child has a relatively immediate access to the benefit of that saving. Although saving is still not spontaneous, its functional value becomes apparent to the child in the very real sense that it allows future consumption. While we have talked about approaches to children's saving as perhaps being motivated by a desire to educate their children in the function and value of saving many parents may be motivated by far more short term concerns to encourage their children to save. They may not be rich enough to provide a financial cushion for the child's future or privileged enough to use pocket money as a means of educating the child. Their reason for encouraging saving may be far more practical; so that the child can buy presents that the parents cannot afford to buy, for example.

Again, we must stress that our sample of parents were mostly middle class. One would expect the income constraints on the parents to influence the child's economic socialisation more in a family where those constraints are tighter. Certainly for this particular mother the child's saving served an immediate economic function for both herself and the child:

> MS F: "Not because I'm a great believer in saving money, because I'm not sure that I am, but I think more for practical reasons. Perhaps because it suits me, as I say, because I can't afford to buy them things . . ."

Avoiding Temptation by Withholding Money. In one family a completely different approach was used to regulate the child's finances. This involved the complete withdrawal of all monies from the children in an attempt to promote behaviourial change and social learning. There were four children in this particular family and the eldest had been involved in taking money from the house and spending it on fruit machines. The parents (who argued that children could not engage in the adult financial world) reasoned that the best way to stop their child behaving in this way was to stop his access to money:

> MR. O: "But it puts you in a funny sort of dilemma really because you, as you say, you're being cruel to be kind, but I seriously and firmly believe that the children are happier with nothing. They don't, and we've found in the past it's been a huge mistake to try and bribe them or, you know, you can't buy them off. They have nothing, and they are going to do things not because they get 50p or £1 but because you tell them to."

Withholding money thus "protects" children from issues of choice; is part of a grander scheme of parental power where children do things by directive; and finally, disempowers the child by making them absolutely dependent on parents for even the smallest item. This approach marks the most authoritarian approach to the management of a child's finances reported by any parents in the study. Apart from the immediate effects on the child's economic status it is hard to see how this approach could engender an understanding either of the function of saving or its value in more absolute terms.

Children's Saving in Banks and Building Societies

There is however a type of saving other than pocket money saving going on. It is saving by parents on behalf of their children. In the same way that parents provide small amounts of spending money for their children as pocket money, so they employ "saving schemes" on behalf of their children. The money that is saved in this way, usually in building societies on behalf of their children, is described differently. It is, so parents report, appreciated as different from pocket money by their children:

MRS. S. "But they understand that that's different money. That's not money for spending, that's money for saving."
Q. "For a rainy day?"
MR. S. "Well it's till they are old enough to appreciate that amount of money, and then they can just have it. I would expect they would use it wisely then."

Giving Children Nominal Control of Their Bank Account.   Although most parents did open bank or building society accounts in the names of their children very few did it without their children's involvement. Most parents chose to give the child nominal control over the money. These accounts were opened in the child's name and the process of saving involved the child going to the bank to deposit money at regular intervals. But how might this approach help the children develop an understanding of the value and function of saving? Certainly as an approach it provides a combination of future wealth together with a rather restricted form of economic experience. This type of experience could serve a number of different functions in the context of economic socialisation. First, it provides the ideal opportunity for the parents to discuss the functions of saving. Second, and relatedly, it brings the child into contact with information on the value of saving provided by the marketing industry. Third, it provides practice in actually going to the bank and so encourages future confidence in money management. Fourth, it might provide the basis of a savings habit.

What becomes clear is that while it is important that the money saved should be nominally their children's own money, their children need have no choice over how it is used. What is important is the habit of putting money in the bank and seeing the money in the account grow. It is almost as if the children were practising saving without any understanding of the functions that the saving behaviour fulfils. Saving is valued in and of itself. But this approach to economic socialisation leaves the child with no evidence of the practical benefits of saving. The children in this situation made no real choices between the present and the future as the money was never really under their control and they could never really recognise the benefits of saving until in retrospect they might admit that mum, and the banks, were right after all.

Clearly parents need to balance this type of abstract knowledge about the role of saving as providing for the future with a more practical type of short term practice in saving. A truly functional understanding of saving can only be established when the choices to save are made by the child and the benefits are obvious over the short to mid term. That is to say the wealth generated by saving is disposable.

Giving Children No Control Over Savings.   For a small number of the parents, saving was invariably done by themselves for the children so as to provide a small financial cushion for later life. The saving was not designed to be instructive, to instil a savings habit or ethos, but to provide for the children materially at a later stage in life. Indeed on one occasion, money given to the children for birthday/Christmas, which may be a substantial sum, was "sequestrated" by parents and put into these long term savings accounts:

> MR. O. "I think they accept that it's something where, occasionally money comes their way, and it has to go into the savings account and they accept that's money for the future. I've told them it's for, the money is for them, when they leave home."

But for some parents, it is possible to see an intertwining of pocket money and institutional saving on behalf of their children. For example, one parent who did not at present give his children pocket money could foresee this scenario:

> Q: "Can you foresee a time when you might start giving pocket money?"
> MR. E. "I'm not quite sure to what extent we'd always want to be doing it in terms of cash rather than saying, 'look we're putting £5 a month into your building society for you', or something like that. I'm not necessarily sure he'd want it in cash, and we'd give him it if he wanted, but we're not very organised about that."

It is clear that for some parents what is more important is the accumulation of a financial base for their children to work from, rather than instilling in them any practices that might in their own right lead to a secure future. Parents take up a role as providers (even if this means "enforced" saving on behalf of their children) rather than as primarily educators. It is their hope that wisdom will be passed on to their children through the child observing the "benefits" in later life, of the parents' action at this time.

PARENTS' VIEWS OF CHILDREN'S ECONOMIC COMPETENCE: SAVING AS AN ANTIDOTE TO ECONOMIC MADNESS

As has been discussed in the previous sections, parents' conceptualisation of children's saving/spending is complex and multifactorial. Children's saving is not simply a matter of hoarding pocket money, but is the subject of negotiation on different levels. Thus, to be able to examine parents' beliefs about children's saving, it is necessary to consider a more general picture of parents' beliefs about children's financial competence. If children were already prudent and thrifty there would be no need to teach them to save. So this broader picture must of necessity include parents' beliefs about why children spend money rather than save it.

The most striking aspect of this broader picture that parents have of the relationship between children and the world of economics is the language with which beliefs about children's spending are expressed. When some of the parents talk about their children's tendency to spend the rhetoric of "disease" and "disorder" creeps into the conversation. Children's spending is often seen as being compulsive and uncontrolled:

> MR. M. "L. is more inclined to have *spending binges*, which we don't stop. She will go out and buy a lot of books and just things that she wants to have, and she will spend all her savings in one go, and well that's all part of the learning process, we don't stop her doing it."

The idea of "spending binges" invokes parallels with compulsive eating, gambling and drinking, and suggests that children lack self-control. This "urge to spend" is conceived of by this particular parent as being without thought, for even if the purchases are "things that she wants to have", the outcome must ultimately be a disappointment for her as it is described as "part of the learning process"; something that can be chalked up to experience. There is for parents an age theory of children's learning, in that it is possible to ameliorate this particular "condition", simply by allowing experience (and by implication age) to take its course. It is not necessary for the parent to institute a bold remedial plan to deal with these "binges", for although the child may lack self control, it will be learned through experience. For other parents however, it is this very lack of worldliness that lies at the root of this abnormal behaviour:

> MR. O. "What happened was, the more money they had, the more *disturbed* they became by the number of things that they could buy with it, and the number of things they then wanted. Whereas if they had no money, they are actually much happier and much more content within themselves, because they can't have anything, so they don't have to *tear their minds apart* wondering what they are going to spend their next 20 pence on."

This excerpt comes in the context of an explanation by a parent about why this child does not get pocket money. The child had previously received pocket money but this had been stopped. Again the explanation of the relationship between the child and a world of money, exchange etc. is couched in language associated with "disorder"; ("disturbed", "tear their minds apart" etc.). Again it is this parent's contention that his child cannot deal in functional terms with money and the world, and that the only remedy, at this time, is to withhold the source (or at least catalyst) of the child's disturbing behaviour. Again, there is not talk of a remedial plan to "instil a habit" for example. An integral part of this rhetoric of disorder is the complementary notion that any saving that is in fact made by the child is not a product of conscious design:

> MR. M: "—so, I'll encourage them to save in order to buy those sorts of things and they do that, but I don't think they do it consciously; they just find they have a surplus at the end of the week which they put in their moneyboxes and it just

accumulates. So I don't think it's a conscious saving although we do talk to them about saving and they find that they have saved this money although they've not consciously done it."

This notion of unconscious saving accords well with notions of uncontrolled spending, creating a picture of children as being played upon by "states of mind" beyond their control. As this parent reports, even discussions about saving with the child do not ameliorate this set of behaviours. The child still continues to save unconsciously. It is a model of the child that sees children as "unsophisticated", "non-rational" and in a sense, closer to a "natural state". On the level of practise however, other conceptualisations of children's saving and how to encourage it emerge. It appears that, in practise, parents work with notions of reinforcement schedules and associative learning, in order, they believe, to foster a savings "habit" or at least good money sense.

These attempts at behaviour modifying strategies are apparent in parents financial provision for their children. For example, one particular family divided up the pocket money allocation they provided, between money for spending and money to go in the bank. On closer examination it emerged that an extra pound had been introduced by parents, from their own money, (Child Benefit, in fact) with the express intention that it should be banked by the child in the school bank on a Monday morning. Their children's standard rate of pocket money was unaffected as there was never any question of that extra pound coming under the control of the child. The parents gave them the extra pound to put into the bank at school as "practice"; to foster a habit of using the bank as a means to learn about saving:

Q: "So the pocket money you give them is designed to go in the bank?"
MRS. P: "Well, no, that's an extra pound."
MRS. P: "Which actually comes out of family allowance."
MRS. P: "I only just recently started that cos I thought it was a good idea to get them used to putting money in the bank."

COMMENT

In contrast to the apparent consensus in the general approaches to encouraging children's saving used by different savings institutions, parental reports suggest a wide range of approaches to their children's economic education. It seems that a surprisingly large number of parents do not make any concerted effort to "train" their children in the management of money, most relying in a rather vague way on encouraging a savings habit either by forcing or encouraging their children to save pocket money or by letting their children have nominal control of a bank account opened in their name. Like the savings institutions there is no attempt to teach the purpose of saving nor the value of thrift as a trait of character.

It may of course be that parents feel that, while it is their responsibility to ensure that money management is taught to the child, the banks and building societies are far better teachers. Saving is certainly more fun with "Woody's wobbly money tree" and the banks appear to have devised a special economic language for children in which interest is a reward for good behaviour.

6

Contrasting the Economic, Social, and Developmental Significance of Young Children's Behaviour

At the end of the last chapter we were faced with an apparent contradiction. On the one hand, the data presented in Chapters 3 and 4 make it quite clear that by the age of 12 children have developed a functional understanding of saving. That is they recognise that saving is an effective way of providing for future expenditure when they are faced with a constraint on income. Or in other words that it forms the basis of good money management. In practical terms they understand that putting money in a bank can serve both defensive (from both external and internal threats) and productive functions (as a means of earning interest). On the other hand, we have shown in Chapter 5 that banks, building societies and parents invest very little time in teaching children about the functional significance of saving. They all seem to rely to a greater or lesser extent on simply encouraging a savings habit in children. So we are left with the question where does the functional understanding of saving displayed by children come from? In this chapter of the book we will try to answer this question. In order to do this we will concentrate on two issues. We will look at the developmental relationship between what we have called pre-functional or habitual saving of younger children and later functional saving. We will also try to isolate the possible role played by social representations of savings originating from parents and saving institutions in this developmental process.

It was suggested in Chapter 1 that a full understanding of the development of economic thought and action requires that we shift from an adult- to a child-centred approach when trying to understand economic development. If we do this we get a very different picture of what to adults (and most psychologists) are apparently irrational and non-functional economic actions. When economic development is understood from the child's point of view we must change from talking about the value of activities defined according to externally imposed "objective" economic standards, to talking about their value on the child's own terms. In other words changes from apparently irrational or non-functional behaviour to rational and functional behaviour should be seen as really only involving changes in the conceptions of the value of actions held by children.

This type of account of the rationality of action leads us, on the one hand, to accept the children's explanations of their choices at face value; from this position the debate about rationality no longer constitutes an empirical issue (Rachlin, 1980). On the other hand, it leads us to make explicit any qualification implicit in statements about the adaptive or functional status of the child's practical actions. In other words, although an action may not serve an economic function it may constitute an adaptive or functional response at some other level.

The conflict between these two approaches to value are nowhere more clearly seen than in two attempts to understand what we have called the pre-functional period of economic development. The first approach might be called the cognitive limitations account. This approach to explanations is typically taken by the cognitive developmentalist theories described in Chapter 1 (see also Chapter 7).

This approach states that a young child's economic performance is governed by limitations in cognitive functioning (Fox, 1978), the economic style of young children being the product of systematic limitations in their ability to reason (Jahoda, 1983). This type of account would suggest that the child's inability to save would be based on some logical deficiency in integrating information about intertemporal relations (e.g. Piaget, 1969; 1970b).

The second approach can be seen as broadly compatible with the socio-developmental approach also described in Chapter 1. This approach presents an alternative to the cognitive developmentalist orthodoxy. It states that the young child's saving behaviour is due to some positive cultural influence established during the process of socialisation (see Goodnow, 1990 for a range of possible mechanisms). In the studies reported in this book, and in previous studies, we have consistently isolated a stage during which children's explanations of economic behaviour suggest, on the one hand, an insensitivity to the economic consequences of behaviour and, on the other, an adherence to the social norms governing economic behaviour (Sonuga-Barke, Lea, & Webley, 1989; Sonuga-Barke, Webley & Lea; see also Furth, 1980). As a result of this we have suggested that there exists a period during development when children assign social rather than economic or financial value to what would normally be considered to be economic actions. Young children valued saving not for the economic function it performed but because it was socially approved of and so rewarded; they saved because saving was presented as a good thing to do in social but not necessarily economic terms. In other words there was a specific reason for the levels of habitual saving found in the experiments in Chapter 3 and (to a certain extent) Chapter 4. The value of the act of saving was not determined by its economic function, but rather because of its status as an acceptable and rewardable social act.

From this position children's failure to engage in functional saving cannot be seen as a product of limitations on economic and social reasoning but rather as the product of socially mediated changes in children's understandings of legitimate or valuable behaviour (Shweder, 1982). This is a more positive account of this period during economic socialisation. On a wider level, this type of approach would view development as a process in which age-related changes in performance are due to the reorganisation of the nature of control exerted during a child's interaction with the social agents and institutions that are, to a large extent, responsible for arranging both the economic and social contingencies controlling young children's behaviour (Valsiner, 1987; 1988) rather than a reorganisation of the child's cognitive structures, as suggested by many of the limitation accounts (Ng, 1983). In short although the economic behaviour of the 6 year olds can be described on one level as maladaptive, on another level it is adaptive in terms of the value derived from conformity to specific social norms. It serves a social function for the child. Perhaps the attempts simply to engender a savings habit form the basis for this period of saving, which we have been right to describe as pre-functional in the economic sense but which is clearly functional in a social sense.

But this still leaves us to solve the riddle of where the functional understanding of saving begins and the nature of its developmental relationship to "pre-functional" understandings of saving.

A child-centred account of economic action views these pre-"mature" conceptions of rational economic action as meaningful to the child. Might they also play an important role in the development of functional saving? Or in other words what is the developmental significance of the pre-mature conceptions of rational economic actions. At this point it is important to draw a clear distinction between economic functions and what we might call developmental functions of actions and understandings.

The economic functions of children's behaviour have been discussed at great lengths and are related to the maximisation of utility by the adaptation to economic constraints. By developmental functionality we mean that responses in some way play an important role in the developmental process (c.f. Flavell & Wholwill, 1969). The importance of this distinction for a theory of the development of economic behaviour relates to the fact that these two forms of functionality, as with social and economic functions of actions, may well be in conflict, i.e. a behaviour might be non-functional in a purely economic sense, but still play an important role in the developmental "progress" toward economic efficiency. In other words some actions may play an instrumental role in the future developments of the child's understanding of the economic world, while hindering that child's short term economic success.

Thus as well as showing that young children's non-functional economic behaviour can be adaptive in a social sense, the child-centred approach suggests that it may well also serve a developmental function. As was suggested earlier, developmentally functional behaviour is that which plays a significant role, in this case, in the development of effective economic behaviour. But how exactly might the period of pre-functional economic behaviour serve a developmental function?

Before we can answer this question we need to make one more distinction. This time between two types of developmentally significant actions. One set of these might be called structurally significant and the other instrumentally significant actions. Most stage or phase theories of development assign developmental significance to non-"mature" stages in the development towards "mature" performance (Furth, 1970; Piaget, 1969). They argue that the vertical structure of sequential development confers structural significance on stages during which semi-stable non-mature performance acts as the basis for, and so is structurally related to, later developments (Flavell, 1971). For instance, Piaget argued that concrete operations in some way develop out of and so are structurally based on the pre-operational structure that existed before.

The significance that a socio-developmental theory of economic development assigns to such transient non-mature stges is quite different. Rather than providing a stage in the developmental structure, they are seen as being instrumental in providing the skills necessary for the future development of practical and economic activity.

The development of effecive saving can be seen in this way; during the period of "pre-functional" saving when high levels of saving that seemed to serve no economic purpose were seen, children were learning how to save; during the second phase they were learning when to save. Put in another way, what can be seen from these studies is that although the economic function of saving was not apparent to the 6 year old children, i.e. their actions did not serve short term economic ends, the children's behaviour did provide the intensive practice in practical responses such as saving, that is essential for the eventual production of effective economic behaviour. During these periods of socially mediated practice young children can explore the limits of their behavourial repertoire, its relationship to certain consequences, and so develop those strategies that research has suggested are essential for the development of effective intertemporal choice (see Rogoff & Wertsch, 1984 for studies of social context in cognitive development).

Obviously the development towards effective economic behaviour cannot be accounted for solely in terms of the development of waiting and saving skills. Although these are essential to the solution of any intertemporal maximisation problem, a relatively sophisticated level of mathematical ability also needs to be acquired, in order to calculate effectively and relate different choice dimensions. Consequently the development of economic behaviour can be seen as occurring on two separate, but complementary levels. Effective economic action requires the development of both practical skills (saving and waiting) and reasoning skills (calculating and comparing).

From this, it can be seen that the period of economic maladaptivity is developmentally significant on both of the levels described. As suggested, it has an instrumental significance in that it leads to the learning of behavioural skills but it can also be recognised that it also has the structual significance suggested by sequential theories of the development of reasoning and cognitive skills.

7

First Commentary

Cognitive Aproaches to Economic Development Revisited

Anna Emilia Berti
University of Padova, Italy

INTRODUCTION

Edmund Sonuga-Barke and Paul Webley's work, which forms the main part of this book, presents a series of ingenious experiments that, by means of play economies, aim at studying whether and how children of different ages manage to save. In these studies, an approach to economic socialisation is proposed, which the authors call "socio-developmental" and which they contrast to the cognitive-developmental approach followed in many investigations on children's economic conceptions. Here, I intend to discuss these two approaches, as defined and compared in this book by the authors.

First, I analyse how they have been characterised; second, I ascertain whether the description of the cognitive-developmental approach is adequate. Third, I clarify the relationships between the two approaches according to the authors. Lastly, I examine the studies included in this book, in order to check whether, and to what extent, their results are clear, convincing, and consistent with the premises.

THE "STANDARD COGNITIVE-DEVELOPMENTAL APPROACH"

The comparison between the two approaches is presented in the premise (Chapter 1) and conclusion (Chapter 6) of the empirical studies. In Chapter 1, the "standard cognitive-developmental approach" label is applied to that part of research on economic socialisation that is firmly based on a Piagetian model.

The authors present it as a fairly straightforward extension of the cognitive-developmental approach into the social economic domain. In their opinion, this approach has a number of characteristics that leave us with only partial understanding of economic development during childhood:

- Economic cognition, rather than economic behaviour, is studied, and the methods are mainly based on verbal reports.
- The stress is upon adults' economic institutions; the economic world of children is disregarded.
- A nominal definition of economic behaviour is used, considering as "economic" such actions as buying, saving, etc., as opposed to playing or talking to friends. The fact that any behaviour can be economic, when it expresses the intention to maximise reward, is not recognised.
- An individualistic view of the causes of development is put forward: children construct their understanding of the complexity of economic relations through individual interactions.
- The fact that economic activities and institutions are means of realising the economic values of a certain society, which are embodied in social representations transmitted to children, is not recognised.

This list might suggest that what the authors call the "standard cognitive-developmental approach" constitutes a rigid and clearcut framework. It is actually a series of studies, started in the Fifties and intensified especially from the end of the Seventies, by various authors, most of whom were psychologists (Danziger, 1958; Sutton, 1962; Furth, Baur, & Smith, 1976; Furth, 1980; Jahoda, 1979, 1981, 1983, 1984; Jahoda & Woerdenbagch, 1982; Berti & Bombi, 1981, 1988; Berti, Bombi, & Lis, 1982; Tan & Stacey, 1981; Ng, 1983; Leiser, 1983; Echeita, 1985; Claar, 1987, Furnham & Cleare, 1988; Cram & Ng, 1989), with some sociologists (Strauss, 1952, 1954; Connell, 1977; Burris, 1983). What these studies have in common is their interest in some kinds of topics and the reference to Piaget's work, which was almost unavoidable in those years. This reference, however, is not always there, and when it is, it is not always in terms of agreement.

The aim of these studies was not to investigate the development of economic competence, trying to find in children the antecedents of adults' economic behaviours, nor was it to study explicitly defined economic cognition. The aim (at least for authors such as Strauss, Danziger, Furth, and Jahoda, who first contributed to developing this field of research) was rather to assess children's knowledge about social institutions: the number of studies on this topic, up to recently almost totally neglected, is even nowadays very small compared to those on physical and mathematical understanding.

The description and ordering of children's conceptions at different ages was necessarily the first step, although this did not prevent the researchers from posing questions on the role of environment and from carrying out some cross-cultural (Tan & Stacey, 1982; Jahoda & Woerdenbagch, 1982; Jahoda, 1983; Ng, 1985) and experimental investigations (Ng, 1983; Echeita, 1985; Berti, Bombi, & De Beni, 1986a, 1986b; Berti & De Beni, 1988) in order to find answers. The most recent research has aimed at verifying to what extent schooling can lead children to a better comprehension of economic institutions (Ajello & Bombi, 1988; Ajello, Bombi, Pontecorvo, & Zucchermaglio, 1986, 1987).

Some authors have recognised that the Piagetian framework only partially fits economic conceptions, and have used it with some adjustments (Danziger, 1958; Furth, 1980; Jahoda, 1984; Berti, Bombi, & De Beni, 1986a). It is possible that the most recent developments in cognitive psychology may offer other frameworks to research on economic cognition. Leiser (1983) has recently interpreted the development of economic notions in terms of Nelson's (1986) script theory; Berti and De Beni (1988) have linked the understanding of the notion of shopkeepers profits to STM capacity, possession of certain logic-arithmetic skills, pre-existing knowledge structures, and access to relevant information. Promising perspectives on the understanding of economic knowledge can be opened by the approach to cognitive development in terms of domain-specific restructuring (Carey, 1985, 1986; Vosniadou & Brewer, 1987), which is providing very interesting results in the field of physical knowledge. Educational research on misconceptions and misrules preventing learners from understanding and acquiring physical, chemical, biological, and arithmetical notions may indicate how to devise effective teaching programmes (see West & Pine, 1985).

THE SOCIO-DEVELOPMENTAL APPROACH

According to the authors' presentation in Chapter 1, the socio-developmental approach focuses on children's construction of their economic world while responding to problems of resource allocation with such activities as bartering, betting, and giving presents, and more generally while solving problems that arise when fulfilling a goal restricted by a choice limitation. In addition, this approach places children within the context of society, trying to ascertain when and how their economic action and understanding are oriented by values embodied in social representations. A series of new questions is thus proposed, and new fields of investigation are opened.

Up to this point, the main differences between the two approaches seem to concern the three following points: (1) investigation content (conceptions on adults' economic world vs children's economic actions); (2) method (interview vs other means of data collection); (3) the role to be attributed to information conveyed by various social agents.

These differences are not sufficient to distinguish two distinct approaches: suffice it to say that, in order to study moral development, Piaget (reference to whose work characterises the cognitive-developmental approach, according to the authors) started from the children's world, that is, from practice and understanding of game rules (Piaget, 1932). Moral development has been studied by means of problems relevant either to adults (Kohlberg, 1976) or to children (Damon, 1977), by two authors who define themselves as cognitive developmental psychologists.

As concerns methods, the interview is definitely not the research tool characterising the cognitive-developmental approach; although it has been widely (but not exclusively) used in the study of economic conceptions, other methods can obviously be used by whoever can devise them. Nor can references to social beliefs and values distinguish one approach from the other: Nobody denies that children receive from adults information that embodies representations built and shared within different social groups, a suggestive study by Connell (1977) proposes that, among the various ideologies present in their environment, children at different ages assimilate those that best fit their intellectual abilities.

In fact, in spite of the authors' critical remarks on the cognitive-developmental approach, they suggest that it is in some ways compatible with the approach they put forward (pp.7–8). Instead, one approach can be distinguished from another by the role attributed to social agents: Do they determine the behaviour of children by giving them information or rewards, or do children actively contribute to their own development by interpreting incoming information according to the knowledge and abilities they possess at a certain age level (not necessarily defined in Piagetian terms)? Furthermore, must we believe that whatever children think and do reflects information received from outside, or must we admit that they can imagine and infer, and even construct ideas not reproducing (or distorting) what has been conveyed to them by others?

The above questions lead us to the real difference between the two approaches, explicitly introduced by the authors only towards the end of their work (but which is more or less implicit in their investigations). In effect, in Chapter 6, the two approaches are explicitly considered "alternative" and characterised according to their theoretical assumptions: the cognitive-developmental approach "states that a young child's economic performance is governed by limitations in cognitive functioning" while the socio-developmental approach:

> states that the young child's saving behaviour is due to some positive cultural influence established during the process of socialisation . . . this type of approach would view development as a process in which age-related changes in performance are due to the reorganisation of the nature of control exerted during a child's interaction with the social agents and institutions that are, to a large extent, responsible for arranging both the economic and social contingencies controlling

young children's behaviour . . . rather than a reorganisation of the child's cognitive structures as suggested by many of the limitation accounts. (Pp.86–87).

This quotation suggests that the alternative put forward is none other than that between cognitive psychology and a traditional view of behaviourism. As the debate on these two approaches is long-lasting and has had contributions, on both sides, from very influential authors, I will not linger on the reasons why I prefer the former to the latter. Rather, by a thorough examination of the studies presented, I intend to show how the authors' behaviouristic approach is a hindrance to the investigation of the themes they themselves suggest, due to the aprioristic restrictions imposed on the explanation of the development of economic thought and behaviour.

BOARD GAME PLAY ECONOMIES

The aim of the first two studies is to investigate the precursors of saving, which, according to the authors, are the following: (1) understanding of the inclusive nature of economic actions; (2) understanding of the concept of "temptation"; (3) the ability to use strategies to cope with temptation (incidentally, this list has a fairly cognitive flavour!).

The procedures adopted are very ingenious and appear suitable to the authors' aim. The limitations of verbal methods, especially when small children are involved, are generally recognised, and much progress in cognitive developmental research has followed the devising of tasks in which children were required to act rather than speak (Gelman, 1978). The results are suggestive: we can see that none of the 4 year olds, some of the 6 year olds, but all of the older children understand that losing money (either by spending it or by being robbed) affects future opportunities to buy. The notion of temptation has different meanings at different ages, and the strategies to cope with it follow a trend from overt to mental actions. However the authors, rather than focusing on these age-related changes and furthering research in this direction, devote the following experiments more and more to the problem of token saving, perhaps because it better fits their theoretical framework.

We see that, in Studies 1 and 2, the 4 and 6 year olds lose many of their tokens, either because they are robbed or because they spend them. Their use of the saving boxes, although frequent, is not functional, and they are unable to explain its purpose. According to the authors' interpretation, children practise such "non-functional saving" because they give saving a positive value although they do not understand its economic function; this is attributed to the fact that they were taught the value of saving as a social goal without an explanation of its functions.

This interpretation appears to me rather questionable: It is not clear to what extent children's use of the saving boxes reflects their behaviour in everyday life, rather than their commitment to the rules of the game. Piaget (1932) has shown that, up to the age of 7/8 years, children follow the rules as best as they can and regard them as unchangeable, although they sometimes do not understand their purpose.

More generally, justifications of actions on the part of young children in terms of moral obligation have been found in several domains: economy (see Berti & Bombi, 1988; Furth, 1980; Jahoda, 1981, 1984), social convention (Turiel, Killen, & Helwig, 1987), and event representation; young children have a tendency to equate "the way it is" with "the way it should be" (Nelson, 1986). This tendency has even been found in children's explanations of natural phenomena: the sun, for instance, cannot go down at midday, because "it has to shine all day long" (Piaget, 1926). Various more or less convincing explanations for this sort of answer have been put forward within cognitive-developmental theories. Whenever such an answer is found, we cannot forget its ubiquity, and give it a local interpretation that refers solely to a specific social influence.

Experiment 3 aimed at explicitly testing the hypothesis that young children understand the value of action in social terms and older children in terms of economic consequences. Six- and twelve-year-old children were therefore faced with choices between actions that were socially positive but economically negative, and actions that were socially negative but economically positive. This ingenious experiment is elegant, and its results are suggestive and intriguing. The interpretation put forward by the authors—that 6-year-olds do not regard actions in economic terms but in terms of social value based on social representations—is plausible, but the data allow other interpretations that must therefore be checked.

A first consideration that comes to mind is that a negative evaluation of theft does not necessarily derive from social representations; being robbed is undoubtedly unpleasant, and children might have experienced something similar ever since the first time somebody took a toy away from them. Secondly, I wonder whether the choice between paying a toll and being robbed was actually made by taking into account the costs of the two alternatives, namely, by considering both kinds of value involved (i.e. social, or possibly psychological, vs economic).

This might well have been the case. However, answers based on only one of the two or more dimensions involved in the task material have often been found by Piaget and other authors. The most obvious case is conservation: young children required to make judgements about a certain amount of liquid pay attention only to its level, failing to consider its width.

Piaget interprets these answers in terms of lack of logical structures: pre-operational children cannot multiply asymmetrical relations. Robbie Case (1985) has found the same phenomenon in a wide variety of tasks, regarding not only physical, but also social, spatial, arithmetical, linguistic and other domains. In the theory put forward by this author, a central role is played by working memory capacity, whereas Piaget's logical structures are substituted by domain-specific problem-solving procedures.

SAVING IN A PLAY ECONOMY AND IN REAL LIFE

The fourth study was carried out with two distinct aims: 1) to create a more realistic "artificial" economy in which to assess more cogently the result of the previous three studies; 2) to provide a "salient environment in which participants could be asked about the real-life equivalents of the situation presented. In other words, the participants' understanding of the play economy were used to gain access to beliefs and behaviours so difficult to study with children in a real-life situation" (p.44). This second aim appears at times to prevail over the first: ". . . in the present study the actual behaviour in relation to the bank is not as important as the opportunity to interview the children *in* the bank environment about their understanding of banks and bank-related strategies."

This statement strikes me as implying that, in order to gain access to children's beliefs, interviews should be carried out within a framework parallel to the topic of the questions. If this were the case, such a statement should be justified, because it involves quite strong consequences: on one hand, the (numerous) studies conducted by interviewing children where it is easier to find them, that is at school, are delegitimated; on the other hand, suitable environments are needed, which might be rather expensive in terms of money and facilities. I will postpone this point to the last section, where it will be discussed in the framework of analysis of the data on children's understanding of banking.

In the present section, I deal with children's behaviour in the play economy, first by examining it, and then by comparing it to that observed in the previous three studies. Lastly, I check whether and how it corresponds to the children's everyday saving behaviour as described by the children themselves and by their parents (whose reports are presented in Chapter 5).

Study 4 differs from the previous three not only because of the more realistic situation, but also because the children are facing a different task. In the earlier studies, they had a certain number of tokens from the beginning and had to avoid losing them either by spending them or by being robbed; here, they received tokens each day and have to "put by" a stated amount. A central point, in my view, is whether or not the children knew from the start of the game how many tokens they would receive.

According to the description furnished in Chapter 4, the children (6-, 9- and 12-year-olds) were told that they would get 10 tokens each day. Then they had to choose a toy, and were told that, in order to take it home, they would need to have 70 tokens left. Lastly, a bank account with 30 tokens in it was opened. In short, my impression is that the children were never explicitly told that they would receive a total of 90 tokens and that, as a consequence, they should not spend more than 20 if they wanted to buy the toy. If it is so, the children could only get such a crucial piece of information through a sequence of arithmetical operations, namely, by multiplying the tokens received each day by the number of days, adding the number of tokens found in the account, and finally subtracting the price of the toy.

I suspect that such a sequence of operations exceeds the arithmetic abilities of 6-year-olds, who therefore could not know how many tokens to save. This—and more generally poor arithmetic knowledge—might be one explanation (although not the only one) of the attempts found in some 6-year-olds to save by spending only half. This appeared to the authors to be based on a vague idea that, if you don't spend very much money, you ought to be able to have enough money left.

Another point that attracted my attention was that, during Experiment 4, the 6-year-olds acted differently from their counterparts in the board games; as we have seen, the latter used the saving boxes as frequently as older children, leading the authors to introduce the notion of non-functional saving. In Experiment 4, some 6-year-olds spent all their tokens, whereas others spent only half of them each time. From the age of 9, the children succeeded in saving the money needed, showing that they had arithmetic skills and planning ability and, as pointed out by the authors, they were able to understand that what they were playing was a "saving game".

As regards behaviour in everyday life, assessed through questions asked during the game, the authors state that "What is clear from discussions with the children in this study is that they do engage in complex saving and spending strategies each and every day of their 'economic' lives" (p.50). However, from what follows, I get the impression that these children do not save at all and that the strategies they use deal with spending rather than saving: some suggested that their parents would top up any money saved so that a prize toy could be afforded; the others did not save at all, relying on their parents or on larger amounts of income arriving on birthdays from grandparents and so on. In Chapter 5 we are told by these children's parents that they spend all the pocket money they give them.

Some actions observed in the play economy (spending all the tokens, spending only half, asking the experimenter to top up), may easily be understood, as proposed by the authors, in the light of what occurs in everyday life. However plausible this interpretative hypothesis may be, it needs support from correlation between the data about pocket money management in real life and the use of tokens in the game.

In conclusion, the behavioural responses observed during Study 4 only partially correspond to those found in the previous experiments: while 9- and 12-year-olds appeared successful in all the tasks, 6-year-olds' behaviour varied in the different situations: during the board games they used the saving boxes as often as the older children, although in a non-functional way; in the more realistic play economy and in real life they saved little or nothing. In real life, it appears that nearly all the subjects of Study 4, independent of age, spend all their pocket money. This leads me to presume that the behaviours observed in the various experiments reflect different psychological processes; the relation between such behaviours and those occurring in real life remains to be clarified.

THE DEVELOPMENTAL TRENDS AND THEIR EXPLANATIONS

In spite of these inconsistencies, the authors claim that the data from their studies converge to suggest the existence of two developmental trends: (1) a move from non-functional to functional understanding of saving; (2) a move from defining the value of action in social terms to defining it in economic terms. It appears to me that such a fit can be claimed by considering only the verbal replies of the fourth study and disregarding the behavourial ones; the authors do stress that only the older children understood how a bank works, thus showing functional comprehension, whereas 6-year-olds did not. Stated in these terms, the agreement between the two types of study is not founded on a precise correspondence, but on the fact that the terms "functional" and "non-functional" are used to characterise in one case actions, and in the other thought or understanding. The two trends thus acquire a wide and at the same time vague meaning, which paradoxically recalls the interpretative logic based on gross mental features (e.g. egocentrism) characteristic of the early Piagetian theory (Piaget, 1923; 1924; 1926).

As the trends are presented in this way, it appears to me very difficult to explain them in terms of reorganisation of the nature of control exerted during children's interactions with social agents and institutions. Such a task is made even more difficult by the fact that publicity and promotional material aimed at young savers by some banks and building societies (Study 6) and the interviews of most of the subjects' parents (Study 7) did not support this interpretation. In fact, analysis of the promotional materials led the authors to conclude that "there is little attempt to present any explicit view of either the functional or categorical value of saving . . . any explicit emphasis on the moral dimension to saving is conspicuous by its absence" (p.72). However, a little later they claim that "such vested interests determine children's understanding of saving because to some extent they control the types of images of saving available to children" (p.73). In addition, the children's parents appeared to consider pocket money as an opportunity for their children to learn in the area of spending rather than in the area of saving. What most parents did was to open bank accounts on behalf of their children, often giving them nominal control over them. We are not told whether this occurred in different ways at different ages, which may be a plausible explanation for developmental trends in saving.

Although the Studies 6 and 7 do not help to account for age-related changes, they are intrinsically interesting. Analysing the types of economic information available to children (and for that matter to adults) is certainly relevant to an understanding of economic thinking and behaviour, and research on this issue is undoubtedly scarce (but see Connell, 1977; Berti, in press). The three types into which the authors classify the information conveyed by promotional materials (i.e. categorical definition of value; description of the purpose of an action; description of aspects of institutions) should be considered by anybody who, within any approach, is carrying out an analysis of information about economic actions.

Interesting though they are, Studies 6 and 7, as already seen, do not show those changes in social control and social representations that, according to the authors, should explain the move from the "pre-functional" to the "functional" stage. At this point, a new notion is introduced, i.e., that of behaviour which is not functional in an economic sense, but which may be seen as instrumental in providing the skills necessary for the future development of practical and economic activity. According to this view, pre-functional saving provides children with intensive exercise in practical responses and thus allows them to learn how to save, whereas during the functional stage they learn when to save.

It is not clear to me why this account should be considered socio- as opposed to cognitive-developmental, although outstanding theories of cognitive development based on the notion of hierarchical integration of skills do exist (see Case, 1985; Fisher, 1980). However, the main point is that, as we have seen, a high level of saving was found in the youngest subjects only during the board games; in addition, the literature on saving reviewed in Chapter 2 showed that the younger the children, the less they save. As a consequence, non-functional saving can hardly be regarded as characterising a phase in the development of children's economic behaviour.

CHILDREN'S CONCEPTIONS OF BANKING

I now discuss the second aim of Study 4, that is, the construction, through a play economy, of an environment parallel to the real one, in which to interview children about pocket money, saving and banking. I will now try to answer the question deferred earlier: what are the benefits of creating a framework where environment or actions simulate real-life situations about which children are being interviewed, considering its cost in terms of time and facilities? The authors do not make any explicit statement. The answer may be that this procedure might encourage richer and more reliable replies, either by increasing children's motivation to interact with the researcher, or by furnishing them with relevant retrieval cues.

In my personal experience and to my knowledge derived from the literature, children usually have no problems in letting themselves be interviewed and from the age of 6 onwards they have no difficulty in focusing on the topic about which they are questioned. Younger children have a tendency to wander off the subject, but a skilled interviewer, adopting simple devices such as, for instance, the use of pictures as starting stimuli, can obtain interpretable answers even from preschoolers. As to retrieval cues being supplied by the context, although this is generally possible, it appears to me debatable in the present case. In fact, given that the questions being asked were about pocket money, saving and banking, the context may have acted as a retrieval cue under two conditions: (1) the actions performed in the play economy were construed by the children as analogous to those carried out in real life with their own money. As already seen, the data did not support this parallelism, but possibly the contrary. In any case, if we do not trust the answers given by the children on their use of pocket money, their parents can be interviewed; (2) the ideas assessed during the interview were constructed during direct experience of the institutions simulated in the play economy. More specifically, a play bank could act as a retrieval cue on condition that children's ideas about the bank had been constructed during their personal experience. This condition does not appear to be fulfilled, as I will try to demonstrate presently.

In any case, whether interviews on economic questions are better carried out at school or in the framework of a play economy is an empirical issue, which can be resolved only by comparison of the data collected by the two procedures. Therefore, I will now compare children's ideas on banking, as described in Study 4, with those described in cognitive-developmental research. The authors' data can be synthesised in two points: (1) 6 year olds either do not know the functions of the bank, or they think that it is for keeping money safe from other people; (2) from the age of 9, interest on deposit accounts starts to be mentioned. Let us now examine the data found in studies on banking carried out within the cognitive-developmental approach, and how they can be interpreted.

Jahoda's (1981) and Ng's (1983) investigations and the stage sequence put forward by the former on the basis of 11- to 16-year-old subjects' answers have already been described in Chapter 2 of this book, and I will not repeat them here. Instead, I will describe the data on 4- to 11-year-old children, which emerged from other studies in which I myself participated (Berti & Bombi, 1988). They are a group of studies on children's economic conceptions, in which beliefs on banking were expressed during interviews both on this and on various other topics (such as work and payment for it; how grown-ups get money; the concepts of wealth and poverty; buying and selling; means of production and their ownership).

What comes to light from this group of studies is that the very first conception, found in 4 year olds, depicts the bank as a source of money from which anybody can draw. Only later, i.e. at around the age of 6, does the idea that the money drawn out has either previously been deposited or represents payment for some work. Who the bank should pay for a job carried out somewhere else is unclear to children, and perhaps for this reason even at 8 years of age they mention the bank as a providential source when they are asked how employers get the money to pay their employees. In addition, these studies show that up to the age of 10 children believe that the principal function of a bank is to protect money from thieves; many of them do not know about interest, and some even believe that depositors have to pay for this protection.

Bank loans are mentioned from the age of 10, but initially children do not connect money deposited with money loaned: the former is locked away in the safe and returned to the owners when they go to draw it out; the latter comes from various sources—other banks, the state, the local council, taxation. Only at 11 do children say that the bank lends deposited money. Interest is rarely mentioned, and mainly by older children. This topic was dealt with by Jahoda, who found only in some 14- and 16-year-olds the understanding that interest on loans is higher than on deposits, so that the bank makes a profit.

As may be seen, these data fit those described in Sonuga-Barke and Webley's studies, but are more detailed and provide a framework within which the latter can be included. Conceptions about banks appear to develop along a lengthy route, which cannot be reduced to a sequence of only two phases; 8 levels can be identified by joining these data with Jahoda's. How can we explain the move from one to another?

Only tentative hypotheses can be put forward at the moment. In some cases, access to certain information appears to be the determining factor. For instance, mentioning loans later than deposits may be due to the fact that children have more occasion to hear their parents talking about depositing into and drawing money out of the bank than about borrowing, thus coming to know about the former earlier than the latter. The same applies to knowledge about interest. As regards the connection between deposits and loans, we might ask ourselves whether it derives from factual information acquired only from the age of 11, or from reorganisation of children's ideas, made possible by more abstract thinking (e.g., the money drawn out by depositors need not be materially the same, it is enough for the amount to be the same) and by the ability to connect various notions (e.g. those regarding deposits and those regarding loans) into a coherent system. I find the second hypothesis more plausible: there is no social agency in Italy explaining to children from the age of 11 how a bank uses the money deposited in it.

The understanding that interest on deposits is paid using that received from loans and that the latter is higher, thus allowing banks to make a profit, can also be better explained in terms of cognitive restructuring. The difficulties hindering such restructuring are amply and well discussed by Jahoda (1981; 1984), and I will refer to only one of his arguments. In his opinion, children do not differentiate the societal from the interpersonal domains, thus applying to the former the equality and reciprocity rules governing the latter. This difficulty in differentiating is partly due to the fact that children receive factual information about the existence of economic institutions and the activities within them (producing goods, selling, supplying services), while their governing rules are never explicitly stated. Children therefore apply to the societal domain the rules that they themselves experience in the interpersonal domain. Among friends, or between parents and children, there is reciprocity in giving and taking, and a balance is sought rather than something more.

CONCLUSION

One result from these Italian studies that, in my opinion, deserves attention is that no child, at any age, explicitly confers on the bank the function of helping its customers to resist temptation to spend their money; from what children say, and from what they do not say, it appears that they are not puzzled that people neither spend their salary all at once as soon as it is received, nor carry on their person all the money they possess every time they go out. This is hardly surprising: it is the way things work in most families. Hence the need to keep money in a safe place. Whether these children established a relation between saving and banks is not clear. Sonuga-Barke and Webley dealt with this point by asking Study 4 subjects "Do you think a bank helps you to save?" Children's replies showed that, from the age of 9, putting money into a bank was considered as a temptation inhibiting strategy "cos you can never get in to take your money out" (p.58). It is not possible to establish whether there is a real difference between English and Italian children, as the former were explicitly asked about the usefulness of the bank for them, whereas the latter were asked about the bank's functions in general, and all their answers focused on the world of adults.

All this suggests several questions: when and how do children conceive adults' saving? When do they understand that adults may not only have some money left (because they cannot, or do not want to, spend it all as soon as it is received) but also may deliberately renounce spending at the time so as to accumulate money, for thrift or in order to buy expensive goods or as a consumer good itself? What relations exist among the ideas of saving held by children at different ages and from different social backgrounds, adults' current beliefs, and the theories of saving in force either at the present time or in the past, well described in Chapters 2 and 5? These questions are not answered by any of the studies on children's economic conceptions carried out up to now.

One hypothesis suggested by the data so far available is that younger children, believing in easy access to money, do not conceive the idea of saving. Whether it is true or not and, if it is true, how these ideas change with age, is for future research to answer. In general terms, similar questions characterise a current line of cognitive research, which is highlighting some parallelisms between conceptual development in individuals and the history of scientific theories (see Carey, 1985; Confrey, 1990; McCloskey, 1983): the foundations for this line of research were laid by Piaget's genetic epistemology (Piaget, 1925; 1950).

These data and my discussion are intended to suggest that children develop ideas on institutions they do not directly experience, and on economic activities they do not practise themselves, and attribute to them aims and values not always coinciding with those intended by our culture and embodied in social representations. Children acquire information on the existence of economic institutions and activities independently of information on economic aims in general and on those of such institutions in particular. For instance, they know that factories exist before knowing that they produce goods and earn their owners money (Berti & Bombi, 1988; Berti, Bombi, & Lis, 1982); they believe (even at the age of 13) that the producers of certain goods strive to earn enough to live on, rather than to maximise their profits (Berti & Grivet, 1990).

In order to understand children's ideas we must first accurately describe them and then interpret them through any helpful theoretical tool without avoiding a priori references to cognitive constructs and without underestimating the influence of the social environment. There is no doubt that children are affected both by the beliefs and ideologies circulating in society and by the action of various agencies, among which schooling plays a critical role, for what it teaches and how, and for what it does not teach.

Following Sonuga-Barke and Webley's suggestion of investigating the economic world of children—that is, how they act both in managing their money and in making choices about other kinds of resources—may greatly enlarge our knowledge of the relations between children and economy. This subject is in itself noteworthy and can further supply suggestions on the interpretation of children's idea of the economic world of adults. The proposal of Sonuga-Barke and Webley therefore makes an important contribution to a wider perspective on this field of research. However, the interpretative framework must not be restricted within a behaviouristic approach, because this runs the risk of depriving this kind of research of contributions available from cognitive psychology and its most recent developments.

8

Second Commentary

How and Why Children Save

Sharone L. Maital
National Institute of Child Health and Human Development,
Washington, D.C., U.S.A.

Shlomo Maital
Brookings Institution
Washington, D.C., U.S.A.

INTRODUCTION

The adjective and noun that comprise the main title of this interesting book—*Children's Saving*—bracket what we believe are two of the leading issues in modern economics. The first is "economic socialisation"—as the authors put it, how children of different ages solve practical economic problems of workaday life, or, as Brim (1966, p.5) has defined it, "how children are taught to get the work of society done" in the economic realm. The second is society's present–future choice and its reflection in personal and national savings. The largely unexplained decline since 1973 of five percentage points in the fraction of GNP that countries save, in virtually all the Western nations (including the United Kingdom and United States), has put saving behaviour at the centre of economic debate.

The two issues are of course closely linked. Attempts to understand the decline in saving among adults without first learning precisely how and why children save—how they acquire the concept of saving, the value of thrift and the behaviour of setting aside income rather than spending it—have largely failed. Saving and economic socialisation are also linked in another sense. Saving behaviour reflects a close, complex and fascinating interaction between individual characteristics and social and historical contexts, more than any other aspect of the development of economic competencies in children. For this reason, in order to fully understand both the microeconomics and macroeconomics of saving, and perhaps to devise efficient policies to stimulate it, economics and psychology must cooperate effectively—as indeed they do in this book.

Children's Saving, like all good, innovative research, raises as many questions as it answers. In this commentary, we propose to discuss several major issues. The first is how best to *model* economic socialisation in children. In particular, we will discuss the contrast between the cognitive model and the socio-developmental approach favoured by the authors, and propose a synthesis of the two within the framework of Bronfenbrenner's "ecological" paradigm. Second, we will discuss the issue of cross-cultural research—the generality of the authors' findings derived from the study of young children and their parents in the United Kingdom, across different countries and cultures. Next, we will examine an important psychological variable closely related to saving behaviour—the ability to defer gratification—and some related empirical results.

We then proceed to discuss the authors' portrayal of the child's saving decision as an adaption to "income constraint", and offer an alternative formulation, one that sees saving itself as the result of a form of welfare-improving self-imposed constraint, in the framework of a two-self model of behaviour. Finally, the last section deals with the policy implications of the authors' findings, especially in the context of the lack of knowledge and information about economic concepts and institutions that characterises both children and their parents in many countries.

THE THEORY OF ECONOMIC SOCIALISATION AMONG CHILDREN; TOWARDS AN ECLECTIC ETHOLOGICAL APPROACH

Lord Kelvin once asserted that "theory begins with measurement". Purist adherents of the scientific method reverse Kelvin's maxim. But in trying to understand the complexities of behaviour, direct observation is a rich source of good theoretical leads. The interesting measurements Sonuga-Barke and Webley have supplied on the nature and dimensions of present–future choice among children, add important new evidence and theories in supplying Economic Man's missing childhood.

"Economic Man," we observed a decade ago, "is an obstetric marvel. He or she springs to life full-blown, with boundless intelligence, vast experience and sweeping knowledge, all sufficient to enable the solution of the most complex problems of optimal choice under constraints without error." (Maital, 1982, p.24).

Architects and civil engineers would never attempt to master the construction of buildings solely by looking at drawings or at completed ones, without long and hard study of the process through which buildings rise from their foundations. But for years economists felt they could understand fully "how people live and work and think in the daily business of life," as Alfred Marshall

(1890, p.1) defined it, without learning how the basic concepts, goals, values and behaviours underlying economic behaviour evolve and develop from early childhood through adulthood. Even those who do not expect real people to behave exactly like Economic Man believe the theories derived from Economic Man must have predictive value. But the anomalous behaviour of spending and saving over the past decade have undercut even that weak prop.

The economic goals, values and habits of adults are, like all behaviour, powerfully shaped from childhood onwards. The way this process takes place is of crucial importance in understanding how mature adults think about saving, spending, investing and working. How each generation transmits its values and experiences to the coming one is a matter of great interest and practical importance. Adults respond to their environment in the ways they have seen their parents and peers respond. Like ripples in a pond, the influence of events like depressions, wars, stock market crashes and energy crises extends through time in powerful, transparent waves. Those raised during the Depression recall the hardship and conserve their resources lest it recur, whereas those raised during inflation spend their resources before their value erodes.

Thanks to intensive research on children's perceptions and cognitions in economics, especially during the past 10 years, Economic Man *does* now have a childhood. (See Berti & Bombi, 1981, 1988; Jahoda, 1979; Jahoda & Woerden-bagch, 1982; Leiser, 1983; Leiser, Sevon, & Levy, 1990; Siegal, 1981; Stacey, 1982). Now, Sonuga-Barke and Webley's creative study of saving in children, as a way to grasp how "the formal and the functional, the individual and socio-historical characteristics of action interact during the child's socialisation to economic competence" (p.9), provides not only an interesting theoretical perspective, with some important empirical results, but also a valuable new methodological tool, one that can be replicated with relative ease across different ages and cultures, to study not only saving but a wide range of conceptions and behaviours.

Sonuga-Barke and Webley adopt a *socio-developmental* point of view, which sees economic development as functional expressions of culturally determined economic ideals put into operation using formal means. This model stresses the role of children's peers, authority figures and other persons in the "social construction of the economic aims" (p.8) to which the individuals then applies their developing cognitive understanding.

Thus, the authors see "banking, buying, borrowing and betting simply as formal expressions of the system of values that underlie culture- (or subculture-) specific economic ideals, and as such ... representing more or less approved means of fulfilling those ideals." (p.5).

"The main practical implication of the socio-developmental view," Sonuga-Barke and Webley note (p.6), "is that it encourages us to centre on the child's own understanding of their economic world and the problems presented in it. This involves the recognition that the status of the individual as an economic actor . . . is defined in terms of their response to problems of resource allocation, rather than just in terms of their knowledge about the working of the formal world of grown-up economic systems." Thus, they conclude, for example, that "children's failure to engage in functional saving [is] not seen as a product of limitations on economic . . .reasoning [as the cognitive model would suggest] but rather as the product of socially mediated changes in children's understandings of legitimate or valuable behaviour" (p.87).

The model contrasts with the cognitive approach—specifically, neo-Piagetian theory—that stresses the internal process by which children develop the ability to understand and use a given set of adult economic concepts and how this understanding deepens and matures according to age-related stages. Most of the studies of Economic Man's childhood adopt this paradigm (Berti & Bombi, 1981, 1988; Leiser, 1983).

Thus, *Children's Saving* is an important study, not just for its empirical results but also because it espouses a theoretical paradigm that emphasises the important element of *the changing social context*. This represents a departure from the model that has dominated this type of research in the past.

We shall argue that although the cognitive approaches do not sufficiently consider the social context of behaviour, the socio-developmental model is overly limited, in its consideration of context, by focusing on only one aspect of the *process* of contextual influences—the influence of societal cognitive represen-tations of savings (through parents and advertisements). A more comprehensive set of context processes would include the interacting influences of the objective situation and actual behaviour of others, as well as their expressed beliefs. (Chapter 5). We suggest that the development of economic behaviours like saving may be best explained and researched from a broader, systems view of development, such as Bronfenbrenner's (1989) ecological model. This approach provides a basis for synthesising the interactive influences of both a more complex set of contextual variables and individual developmental processes, such as those emphasised by cognitive developmental theory.

THE ECOLOGICAL MODEL

In the last decade, there has been increasing recognition of the important influence of physical and social contexts of development by various systems approaches (e.g. Bolger, Caspi, Downey, & Moorehouse, 1988; Bronfenbrenner, 1988a, 1989; Cochran, Larner, Riley, Gunnarsson, & Henderson Jr., 1990; Dannefer & Perlmutter, 1990; Horowitz, 1987; Lerner, 1991; Lerner & Kauffman, 1985; Valsiner, 1988, 1987; Valsiner & Benigni, 1986). These approaches all share a holistic perspective and a concern for the processes of interaction among various levels of a complex system involving person and environmental components (Gottlieb, 1991).

Bronfenbrenner's (1988a; 1988b; 1989) ecological perspective is widely acknowledged as a model that facilitates a consideration of properties of the environment as a multi-level system (Bolger et al., 1988; Pence, 1988). An ecological perspective is particularly appropriate to the study of development of complex social behaviours such as saving and other economic behaviours since it accepts and even advocates the integration of interdisciplinary findings and an eclectic approach to research (Pence, 1988). Furthermore, an ecological approach emphasises the importance of the culture-specific meaning of behaviour and the context, not only for social and emotional development, but also for cognition. However, although the culture- and context-specific influences on cognitive processes have been increasingly recognised (Bronfenbrenner, 1989; Laboratory of Comparative Human Cognition, 1983; Valsiner & Benigni, 1986; Valsiner, 1987) this area is less extensively researched. Bronfenbrenner (1989) suggests that "the ecology of cognition and competence remains largely an uncharted domain" (p.209). Bronfenbrenner also offers his process-person-context (PPC) model of development for methodological purposes as a means of enabling researchers to "recognise and to specify the ambiguities of interpretation created by the omission of important elements in the selected design" (Bronfenbrenner, 1988a, p.47).

The essence of the process-person-context model is captured by Bronfenbrenner's (1989) equation:

$$D = F_{t-p}(P, E)_{t-p}$$

where D is the developmental outcome, which is a function F(.) of individual intrapersonal processes P and environmental and contextual influences E operating interactively and in a given time frame. (In the subscript, t is the time of the observed developmental outcome and p are the periods of time during which P and E were operating jointly to influence D.) This equation suggests that aspects of the person, the environment, as well as the processes operating in the interaction of each set of variables, may change from one stage of development to another.

In order to understand how the social context influences development, there has to be a model of the structure of the social system. If the behaviour to be explained is complex, as economic behaviour is, there are likely to be multiple dimensions. It is necessary to follow the transmission of the culture-specific contextual influences from more distal to more proximal settings that directly include the child (Bolger et al., 1988). Bronfenbrenner views developmental contexts as an organised system of "progressively more comprehensive levels" (1988a, p.38) of interrelated social structures beginning with the most proximal interaction setting, the microsystem, and spanning out to include the most distal macrosystem, which reflects over-arching cultural or broadly influential context characteristics. A microsystem (e.g. the family) is defined as "a pattern of activities, roles, and interpersonal relations experienced by the developing person in a given face-to-face setting with particular physical and material features, and containing other persons with distinctive characteristics of temperament, personality, and systems of belief" (Bronfenbrenner, 1989, p.227). Mesosystems, the next level up, involve relations between two or more settings in which the developing person is an active participant (for example, family-school relations). The exosystem is defined by the relations between settings, at least some of which do not involve the developing person directly as a participant, but which influence processes occurring at levels in which the developing child is directly involved (e.g. the relationship between the parents' workplace and the child). The macrosystem reflects the culture-wide patterns of inter-relationships among the various embedded levels of the subsystems. These include, in particular, "the developmentally instigative belief systems, resources, hazards, life styles, opportunity structures, life course options, and patterns of social interchange that are embedded in each of these systems" (Bronfenbrenner, 1989, p.228).

The Importance of Structure

Both within and more importantly between the subsystem levels Bronfenbrenner (1988a; 1989) emphasises the importance of the structure of the settings and the processes that occur in terms of interactions. Various dimensions have been proposed as measures of context, some by those working with an ecological model of development and others borrowed especially from family systems theory. Structural concepts describe the organisational *form* of the system or set of subsystems as defined by the *lines* or *relations* (especially interpersonal relations) that connect the parts to form the whole (Bronfenbrenner, 1988a, 1989; Minuchin, 1974). The structure may be considered in terms of physical characteristics as well as interpersonally defined aspects of organisation.

Bronfenbrenner (1988b) notes that *objective conditions*, and *events* as well as *perceived* relations, occurring in the life of the developing person structure the ecological setting. Variables such as SES, education, the number of people in the particular setting, or the number of different settings or institutions involved in which the same person participates, relative ages of members of the system, the physical placement of the setting in terms of available stimuli, space, climate, and the like, the period of time involved in the setting, and actions and decisions in external structures such as public and private institutions all reflect physical characteristics of the context, in as much as they reflect a unified social reality or common codes for regulating behaviour (e.g. Bronfenbrenner, 1988b, 1989; Pence, 1988). Duhl and Duhl (1981) call these variables *systems resources*.

At the interpersonal level, "Structure refers to the regulating codes as manifested in the operational patterns through which people relate to one another in order to carry out functions" (Aponte & VanDeusen, 1981, p.312).

Variables that reflect how interactions and resources are allocated among system members and among subsystems in a larger system have been termed: alliances or coalitions (Aponte & VanDeusen, 1981; Goodnow, 1988, Minuchin, 1974); and social resource allocation (Dannefer & Perlmutter, 1990). These in turn are described in terms of exchange rules, or rules of access, especially to information (e.g. Bronfenbrenner, 1989; Goodnow, 1988), but also to goods (e.g. Long, Peters, & Garduque, 1985); flow/pattern of relating (Duhl & Duhl, 1981) and continuity versus discontinuity of rules (Aponte & VanDeusen, 1981). Access deals with rules about transfer of resources within and between subsystems, especially things such as information as well as membership in the setting (Goodnow, 1988). For example, Bronfenbrenner (1988a) suggests that the levels of the ecological system are linked hierachically; whereas, Goodnow (1988) suggests the metaphor of "eternal triangles", which allows for direct interaction between the developing child and broader parts of the system, rather than indirect influences mediated by the family. Alliances or links among parts in the system also can be described in terms of networks of relationships or social networks (e.g. Bolger et. al. 1988; Cochran, 1990; Weinraub, Brooks, & Lamb, 1977) and in terms of relative power (Minuchin, 1985) or balance of power. It is significant that the terms and language of the ecological approach rely heavily on economics-based concepts such as resource allocation, exchange rules, alliances, etc., in referring to shared relationships, information and products. This makes it especially suitable for understanding economic socialisation, using as it does the framework of economics itself—allocation of limited interpersonal social and cognitive resources—to study how children learn about the allocation of limited economic resources, both for their own personal budgets and for that of society as a whole.

In the context of children's saving, an example of an ecological model is given in Fig. 8.1. Here, for instance, is an interesting research finding that confirms the usefulness of this model. Galin (1989) found, in her study of 171 Israeli high school students, that the "process of economic socialization is qualitatively different among different social classes." Upper-middle-class students tended to work part-time, save more, and have a more liberal, free-market view of the economic system. Lower-class children, paradoxically, tended to be given their pocket money, and favoured a more controlled, interventionist economic system. Here, the interaction of the young person with the economic system, at the exosystems and mesosystems levels, has clearly influenced the social norms, values and concepts the person has acquired.

Children's saving fits well into the Fig. 8.1 model. From an early age children are confronted with behaviours (usually modelled by their parents) that reflect the macrosystem of surrounding economic ideology and culture (thrift vs. spending, free enterprise vs. planning and the welfare state). Direct learning about saving behaviour occurs at the microsystem level, in interactions with parents, schools, and peers. The degree of congruence between microsystems

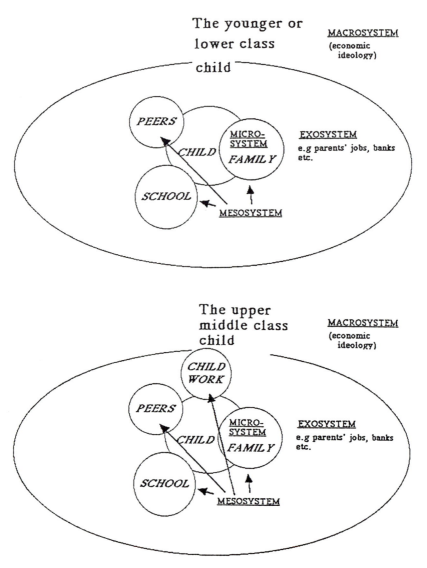

FIG. 8.1. A systematic view of the ecological model: An application to the context of Economic Socialisation. The top diagram shows that the younger or lower class child may be part of fewer microsystems of relevance to economic experience. The more distal parts of the system may be more clearly bounded for this child. The bottom diagram shows that for the older or more middle class child, the world of work becomes part of the microsystems in which the child has direct interactions, leading to more direct influence of the wider levels of socio-economic context on development.

112

coming together to form the relevant mesosystems for a child, may be an important factor in reinforcing habits such as saving in any one microsystem setting. For example, if the child is encouraged to be thrifty and recycle products in school, but the home is not concerned with such saving, the child will be less likely to understand and behave in accordance with a notion of limited natural resources. In addition, areas of experience such as work, may belong in the exosystem for children at one age, only indirectly influencing the child by what parents or other significant adults are seen or heard to do. Then, as the child grows up work becomes one of the microsystems in which the person participates directly. The timing of these changes may vary from one society to another or among different sub-cultural groups, leading to the difference in saving behaviours seen in the example given earlier. There are also important individual differences in the evolving abilities and understanding of the child with regard to the surrounding economic world, which affect the way in which the context influences development in a particular case.

Process variables have been proposed from various theoretical perspectives to explain how behaviour is influenced or how environmental influences are transmitted (e.g. Bronfenbrenner, 1989; Bronfenbrenner & Crouter, 1983). Studies of process are concerned mainly with the relationships between the activities or functions and the goals of the activity. In the context of saving, setting aside resources becomes an act aimed at fulfilling the function of ensuring sufficient resources, for the future. "Rainy-day provision" and "fear of catastrophe" are important reasons frequently given by people for saving. From a developmental perspective, what is of interest is how children translate their construction of the surrounding economic world into action, the process whereby the context influences both the child's understanding of economics and its relationship to behaviour, and the changes that over the course of development throughout the lifespan as both individuals and their contexts change. Sonuga-Barke and Webley's experimental studies begin to address these issues.

In Chapter 4 Sonuga-Barke and Webley note "the possibility that parents can modify the actual economic demands of situations facing children" for example, by "top[ping] up any money the child had managed to save" (p.50), or providing presents, etc. However, they still believe that the "income constraint problem . . . is very real indeed" (p.51) for many children as they grow older. An ecological developmental perspective suggests that issues such as these become hypotheses and the focus of further research, rather than an intervening variable that somehow muddies the results. It suggests the need to study parent-child interactions longitudinally and to compare different social context backdrops in order to gain insight into how and when children develop an awareness of the constraints. It would appear that the child who sees a parent pay for items with a credit card and who is not faced with real limits may develop a view of monetary resources as endless. Furthermore, there may be differences in ability to adapt to the realisation that there are constraints, depending on the developmental stage at which one becomes aware of the constraints. A child faced with constraints from an early age will have a history of being reinforced for waiting and "saving", whereas, the one who has been socialised to relatively few constraints may be more likely to succumb to the use of credit and borrowing at all costs. Such research may help to understand changes in attitudes towards savings that are evident at the macrosystem level.

There is evidence that at the macrosystem level, at least in the United States, there has been a change in beliefs that is reflected both in individual behaviour and in that of government. Surveys suggest that the strong pro-saving value has been weakened by the way households have wrongly encoded the Keynesian prescription. "Saving is stagnant," one woman told a Public Agenda Foundation researcher (Immerwahr, 1989). "If you are buying a lot of products, money is moving through hands, employing everyone, and putting money in the marketplace." Five decades after publication of *The General Theory*, households have encoded the Keynesian message (deficit spending is good when aggregate demand is insufficient but budget surpluses are in order when it is excessive), by shortening it to: spending is good. The devaluation of the future by individuals has not been lost on governments and elected officials, and finds clear expression in the intertemporal choices that are made collectively by legislatures.

How, when and why children have been influenced by this shift in ideology is unclear. It is not without irony that Keynes, whose famous essay *Economic Possibilities of our Grandchildren* (1933) foresaw nearly limitless bounties for future generations, may unwittingly be the cause of the highly constrained futures of those same grandchildren, as the high-spending anti-saving distortion of his theory diminishes the human and physical capital stock passed on to our ancestors.

DO RESULTS ON CHILDREN'S SAVING CROSS CULTURAL BORDERS?

Much research on economic socialisation has focused on the *origins* of economic values: Where do children learn about things like money, banks, wages and prices? How do they acquire their economic values? And how do these values differ across different ages and cultures? Although much of this research has been done on the basis of cognitive paradigms—suggesting that universal processes underlie the understanding of different culture-specific values—many of the results tend to strengthen the validity of the socio-developmental, and ultimately, ecological paradigm. At the same time, such results cast doubt on whether Sonuga-Barke and Webley's findings can be generalised intact to other countries. Sonuga-Barke and Webley themselves note two influences of "social context": the transmission of information about acceptable economic goals and behaviours, and the modification of the types of demands imposed on the child by the economic (income) constraint, each of which may vary in different cultures. The December 1990 issue of *The Journal of Economic Psychology* focuses exclusively on Economic Socialisation and presents results of comparable studies of children aged 8, 11, and 14, in 10 countries: Austria, West Germany, Finland, the U.S.A., Poland, Yugoslavia, Norway, Israel, Algeria, and Denmark. (Leiser et al., 1990). The studies all used a single questionnaire designed by Israeli psychologist David Leiser. They examined children's economic understanding, reasoning and attitudes. The results show how powerfully children are influenced by prevailing circumstances and policies, an influence that may extend into adulthood. These influences are both normative—at the macrosystem level—and behavioural, at the micro- and mesosystem level.

For instance, children in Algeria, France, Poland, West Germany and Norway were asked how people can earn more money. In Norway, three-quarters answered "by strikes". Polish children said, predominantly, by working more, while Algerian children almost never mentioned this answer, instead responding "by changing jobs".

Other studies show that children who helped their parents, in farming and retail trade, in Zimbabwe, understood the profit motive and the working of markets at a far earlier age than comparable children in Scotland, England and the Netherlands. According to Leiser, "children at all ages see the economy as a modifiable system, where enterprise and innovation have their place", including children in Poland—a *smaller* proportion of Polish children thought "opening a factory today" was impossible (9%), than did children from France (23%) and Yugoslavia (35%).

According to Leiser's study, younger children (ages 8 to 11) perceive economic society as a kind of "happy family", in which economic actors "care for one another, factories are created to fulfil existing needs for products, and the government is responsible for making everything work smoothly, giving everyone his due and preventing excesses, etc." In contrast, 14-year-olds perceive the economy as an "instrument", where each individual "tries to interact with the economy to his or her best advantage". For instance, younger children think that factories are opened to give working places and salaries to the poor, and to create output for those who need it. Older children see factories as a source of profit for those who own them.

These cross-cultural results are consistent with the ecological model, which stresses the ongoing, changing interaction between the attributes of the child and the contexts in which development occurs as a function of age and culture-specific context. They illustrate the need to treat culture from a developmental perspective as a dependent or an intervening variable as suggested by Valsiner (1988). The game board and bank simulations devised by Sonuga-Barke and Webley and their sensitivity to children's construction of the particular economic world to which they belong make this a most suitable approach for cross-cultural research. However, the results need to be understood in terms of the culturally-specific meanings that define the context in which the children studied were raised. We would hope that by using these methods with the same children longitudinally and across different cultures, we may gain further insight into developing economic behaviour as a response to social and developmental conditions.

WILLINGNESS TO DEFER GRATIFICATION AND SUBJECTIVE INTEREST RATES: PSYCHOLOGICAL FOUNDATIONS OF CHILDREN'S SAVING

While as Sonuga-Barke and Webley note (p.12). Freud may have discussed saving as "a descendant of anal retention", elsewhere he presented a remarkable formulation of present–future choice as the basis of maturity and of civilisation itself. In his essay *Formulations on the two principles of mental functioning* (1911), Freud describes the two warring principles within us, the pleasure principle (the insistent demand for immediate gratification) and the reality principle (the ability to forego immediate gratification, if larger future rewards make it worthwhile). The transition from the pleasure principle to the reality principle, Freud believes, which takes place in adolescence, is a vital step toward maturation and a precondition of civilised society.

Mischel and his colleagues have long studied ability to defer gratification. A variety of studies, including longitudinal panel studies that track the same group of people over long stretches of time, has shown that people's individual interest rates are shaped in childhood and adolescence, remain stable in later life, and differ widely across individuals and cultures. Furthermore, Mischel's work suggests the crucial importance of differentiating between the choice to delay gratification and the ability actually to wait. The choice of a delayed reward over a present one is closely linked with the developing perception of time and the value placed on each of the rewards.

Children's ability accurately to estimate the length of time has been intensively studied. It may be that the major differences Sonuga-Barke and Webley discovered in children's saving, across the age groups they studied,—6, 9, 10, and 12 years—are related closely to time perception. In further research, this variable should perhaps be measured and used to help partition differences in saving behaviour across ages between time perception and other variables.

Subjective Interest Rates and the Value of Delayed Rewards

While standard economic theory asserts that borrowing and lending in capital markets ultimately brings into equality individual rates (the premium attached to an immediate dollar over a deferred one) and market interest rates, empirical research flatly contradicts this. There is strong empirical evidence that for most of us, the subjective rate of interest (what economists term the marginal rate of time preference) *exceeds* the rate of interest, often by a large margin. (Hausman, 1979; Maital & Maital, 1978, 1984; Maital, Maital & Pollak, 1986; Thaler, 1990). Hausman found empirically-measured subjective interest rates as high as 60%. Kurz, Spiegelman, and West offered subjects in the Denver-Seattle Income Maintenance Experiment actual checks, some with current dates and others deferred but for larger sums, and inferred subjects' subjective interest rates from their choices. Subjective interest rates ranged from 60% (for $2,000 household income, and eight years of education, standardised for assets, family size and home ownership), to 22% for households with $15,000 in income and college education. (Kurz, Spiegelman, & West, 1973). Hausman (1979) inferred marginal time preference rates from individuals' choice of energy-efficient (hence, yielding future savings) but expensive (hence, requiring sacrifice of present income and gratification) air conditioners, or cheap energy-inefficient models. He found subjective interest rates ranging from 89% (for $6,000 income class) down to 5.1% for the $50,000 income class. Antonides (1990) inferred subjective discount rates from decisions to scrap durable goods. His estimates range from 10 to 42%.

The economic evidence on differences in the value placed on future reward fits with Sonuga-Barke and Webley's description of children from working class backgrounds, who "may not be taught to place such a high value on distant, and perhaps uncertain rewards, as children from more affluent and economically stable homes. It is not that these children are less able to produce effective temptation inhibiting strategies but rather that they do not get the opportunity to do so." (p.15).

Mischel (1984) presents evidence that an essential factor in the willingness and ability to delay gratification, as Sonuga-Barke and Webley state, is the ability to divert attention away from the arousing properties of the awaited reward. Keeping the goal in mind while attending to less arousing thoughts and actions enhances the ability to delay gratification, as does distracting activity or even ignoring or forgetting the awaited reward.

Bandura (1982) suggests that in order to sustain behaviour leading to future goals, people may need to set intermediate attainable *subgoals*. "If people experience only easy success, they come to expect quick results and their sense of self-efficacy is easily undermined by failure", he suggests (1989, p.1179). Alternatively, if they have a history of failure in obtaining goals, regardless of their behaviour, there may be a situation of learned helplessness and a poor sense of self efficacy. This may explain why children from disadvantaged backgrounds, with fewer experiences in saving and reaping rewards from that behaviour, have a lower sense of efficacy. At the same time, it suggests a more pessimistic view of the developmental trajectory of saving behaviour for those children in the Sonuga-Barke and Webley sample who did not have experience with constraints, since their experience has been one of "easy success" and they may be more likely to have their sense of efficacy in dealing with economic constraints undermined if this does not occur, and there are no other offsetting experiences such as working, as mentioned earlier, in the course of development.

The fundamental empirically-based proposition—that people differ in their subjective rates of interest—along with the need to establish a means of planning and attaining future goals for development of self-efficacy, assigns a central role to self-imposed constraints on spending and precommitment to saving. When the infra-marginal equality of subjective interest rates and objective interest rates does not hold, intertemporal choice is powerfully influenced by the nature and strength of constraints on spending and debt. The focus of a search for a theory of savings then shifts to those constraints, and their origins in childhood.

SAVING: A RESPONSE TO INCOME CONSTRAINTS OR A PRODUCT OF THEM?

"Saving," Sonuga-Barke and Webley note, ". . . is an adaptive response to the income constraint problem" (p.13). Elsewhere: "saving is a functional response to the demands of the all-pervading income constraint". (p.59). In this view, since income across the life cycle is limited in its amount (i.e. constrained), saving is necessary in order to transfer spending power from periods when income is available or plentiful to periods when it is not. To the extent that it serves this purpose well, it is functional.

While this is formally true, saving itself is probably more powerfully influenced by constraints that people themselves devise and create—self-imposed constraints on their desire to spend. It is these precommitment devices that hold the key to understanding saving, we believe, beginning with childhood. Saving, in this view, is the product of self-created precommitment devices or constraints, aimed at fulfilling the function of responding to the "income constraint". It is a result of what Schelling (1984) has termed the intimate contest for self-command.

The standard economic model of choice portrays individuals as deciding how to allocate their income to competing uses, in the presence of constraints that limit their freedom of choice. This method for framing human choice views constraints as *impairing* our wellbeing—the fewer and weaker they are, the better. In contrast, psychologists are keenly aware that many people go to great lengths to limit and control their own choices. The socialisation literature is largely focused on how cultural norms for self control are transmitted from one generation to the next, initially being imposed by adults until the norms are internalised—an important sign of maturity.

"I can resist anything except temptation," Oscar Wilde once remarked. Twelve-year-old Catherine put it far better, in Sonuga-Barke and Webley (p.39): "[Temptation is] when you want to do something that you don't want to do." Behaviour, in this view, is seen as the result of essentially unlimited appetites and wants, which if uncontrolled would be inimical to long-run wellbeing, and hence are placed under restraints, sometimes highly ingenious ones, that check those appetites and help us resist temptations. Skill in creating, implementing and sustaining such precommitments begins in childhood.

The Two-self Model

A fuller understanding of children's saving may help to achieve a better grasp of saving and spending patterns in adults. Current theories of such patterns are in serious conflict with empirical evidence. The still-dominant economic model of saving and spending, a variation (like all economic models) of the "maximisation under constraint" paradigm, is the so-called Ando-Modigliani "life-cycle" model. Thaler's (1990) trenchant description of this model is this: consumers should spend the value of the level annuity, whose principal equals the present value of net assets, present income and expected future income.

This "levelling" model of spending is sensible. But consumers simply do not behave in this fashion. Thurow (1969) showed that people's spending is far more closely related to their current income than it is to "level-annuity" or life-cycle income. "Spend what you make", in Thaler's phrase, seems to characterise behaviour, when non-discretionary saving like pension deductions and mortgage payments (return of principal only) are taken into account. Strong evidence against the life-cycle model is found in recent papers by Courant, Gramlich and Laitner (1986), Carroll and Summers (1989), and Kotlikoff and Summers (1981). It is not, therefore, a good place to begin looking for an explanation for the decline in saving.

Thaler (1990), Thaler and Shefrin (1981), and Shefrin and Thaler (1988) propose a "behavioural life cycle" model in its place. Their so-called *two-self* theory posits a perpetual intra-psyche war between the "*planner*" (saver) and "*doer*" (spender). Saving requires (scarce) mental energy to implement, in the face of temptations to spend. The "*planner*" part of the self invents self-imposed rules to facilitate saving. "The latter source [of liquidity constraints] may well be more important", Thaler (1990, p.203) observes, than those imposed by capital markets. Comments by children in the present book about the use of banks to restrain their spending suggest that the two-self model pertains not only to adults behaviour to also to that of children.

In Maital (1986), a general model of behaviour was outlined in which self-imposed, self-designed and self-regulated constraints are a major source of improvements in our wellbeing. Building on Thaler and Shefrin's theory this paper quoted George Ainslie (1982, p.71):

> A person's immense capacity for self-reward presents him with an equally immense problem of self-control. A person is led by the basic shape of his reward delay function to exploit his sources of reward wastefully. If he does not bind his

reward process to events outside his control . . . his every appetite is gratified, but so quickly that the anticipation which is necessary to harvest full satisfaction from a drive never develops . . . A person can never rid himself of the opportunity for this kind of regression; it must be, like the old idea of original sin, a constant factor in his motivation. He can only control it through adoption of precommitting devices . . . Thus can subtle appetites . . . be understood not as the product of innumerable separate drives but as disciplines we learn to adopt to protect ourselves from runaway self-reward.

Ainslie's view relies on psychodynamic formulations of self-regulation, which view behaviour as driven from within by the pleasure principle while being continually modified by external constraints that are sometimes internalised, and sometimes countermanded. This model accounts for the individual's capacity for self-regulation, the influence of the situation or context in which decision choices are made, and the interaction between self-regulation and situation in determining behaviour. It is echoed in the present book, where interviews with parents speak of "spending binges", and "urge to spend", a kind of rhetoric of disease and compulsion.

Economic policy generally favours the elimination of such welfare-improving constraints, by deregulating markets and industries and making markets as free and unconstrained as possible. This ignores the fact that people have themselves purposely created such constraints to avoid "wanting to do, and doing, what they don't want to do". (Sonuga-Barke & Webley, p.58): "E: Do you think a bank helps you to save? C: Yes, cos you can never get in to take your money out. E: Is that why you put your money in? C: Yes, cos it stops me from spending it.".

A good example is credit cards. Americans are very conservative about spending through incurring debt, and a significant majority has long believed that this is a bad idea. Today, there are over a billion credit cards of all types in America. Buying with a credit card permits the self-delusion that the debt will be paid off at the end of the month—when large bills often enable payment of only a part of it. It also further hides the reality of constraint from children, who, as concrete thinkers, may view the credit card as a virtually limitless supply of money whose source remains mysterious.

Thus, while the conventional model of saving leads policy to focus on such variables as interest rates and improving the liquidity of saving instruments, it may well be that people seek savings instruments that are *less* liquid, enabling them to avoid the temptation of spend, in a manner and purpose not unlike the manner children put their assets into the bank in the present studies.

One of the most curious examples of this is the way Americans use the personal income tax, and Internal Revenue Service, as a major method for transferring income across time periods. Cordes, Galper and Kirby (1990) note that about *three-quarters* (!) of all individual income tax returns in the United States report overpayments of federal income tax. The average amount of overwithholding is about $1,000, and the total sum of overpayments equals about 20% of total tax liabilities.

Why do individuals provide the government with nearly $100 billion in *interest-free loans*? The authors offer empirical evidence that people use withholding to engage in forced saving, enjoying a sizeable refund at a time when they are planning summer vacations. This self-imposed constraint—withholding could easily be reduced—provides us with the resources for future gratification, when we might otherwise use them up in the present. ("We all need ways . . . to cope with liquidity of money and our inability to resist temptation and external threats," Sonuga-Barke and Webley note (p.45) . . . "it may be the case that childish strategies solve the childish problems quite adequately." One wonders whether the 6-year-old strategies were any more "childish", or less practical, than lending to the IRS.)

Sonuga-Barke and Webley, in conducting a content analysis of the "marketers of saving" and their literature, note the predominance of interest rates as a drawing point for savings programs. "There is surprisingly little variety in these adverts," Sonuga-Barke and Webley note (p.68), suggesting the adverts "were not interested in encouraging saving in general" and instead compete for existing savings rather than work to create new ones. If the two-self model—and Sonuga-Barke and Webley's findings about children's savings—are correct, the adverts may be based on a faulty understanding of saving. Appealing to savers with innovative ways for timely saving, temptation-proof, and yet availability of those savings when needed, might be more effective.

ECONOMIC SOCIALISATION: THOUGHTS ON INTERVENTION

Sonuga-Barke and Webley show fairly conclusively that "banks, building societies and parents invest very little time in teaching children about the functional significance of saving. They all seem to rely to a greater or lesser extent on simply encouraging a savings habit in children." (p.85)

Berti and Bombi (1988, p.216), based on interviews with over a thousand children in Italy, found that children's economic concepts are constructed "largely on the basis of information derived from adults and the mass media, rather than the child's own active exploration of the world."

With adults' own understanding of economics very partial and imperfect, and with the media often conveying incorrect information, together with children's very limited active participation in the workaday world, this together implies that children learn little about saving, work, investing, consuming and other topics crucially relevant to their own lives, until well into adulthood. Nor do most of them ever learn about these concepts as part of their schooling.

It is regrettable that one of the subjects used most in our daily lives—economics—appears to be least taught to children either informally or formally.

From an ecological perspective, it appears that economic beliefs that are expressed at a macrosystem level, and implemented in distal subsystems such as the exosytem that represents government, banks, etc., differ from the manifest behaviour of individuals in socialising their children at the proximal levels of direct interaction. Furthermore, contexts in which many of the more complex economic principles are actively played out are relatively far removed from the daily experiences of today's child. While Sonuga-Barke and Webley discussed with parents their strategies for teaching economic concepts to children, they did not relate the strategies of each parent to the behaviour of the children. Future research that provides data such as these will help fill in the missing parts concerning the links between values at the macro level and socialisation of economic behaviour at the micro-level. Nor is economics part of the child's school experience.

In the United States, only about half of all states have a mandate to teach economics in public schools, and only about one in every thirteen school districts in the nation actually does so. In New York State, with one of the most extensive economics education programs, only one school district in six teaches economics.

An innovative educator named Marilyn Kourilsky, at UCLA's Graduate School of Education, believes even young children can comprehend the principles of economics (Kourilsky, 1977). She has developed a pioneering program called Mini-Society for teaching economics to primary school children. In the program, children start businesses, write cheques and use "banks". Kourilsky found that one of every four kindergarten-age children exhibits entrepreneurial ability—but by the time they reach high school age, only one person in thirty has similar abilities. Apparently, schools not only fail to teach economics to children, but also manage to extinguish a large portion of their innate business intitiative and aspiration.

Kourilsky also found that it was not enough to teach economics to third-graders; she had to teach it to their *parents* as well, who often knew less than their children did about markets and prices after their offspring had completed the Mini-Society program. Kourilsky's experience suggests that the Sonuga-Barke and Webley game-board and bank simulations might prove useful, not solely as tools for researching economic socialisation but also as vehicles for improving economic socialisation and teaching it to children. We surmise that the children who took part in this research ended up knowing more about saving than those who did not.

CONCLUSION

In all but one of the twenty four OECD countries, all forms of saving—personal, business and government—expressed as a percentage of income or GDP, were lower in 1987 than in 1973. This decline in saving implies a serious devaluation of the future among countries that comprise 60% of world output. No persuasive explanation or model has yet been advanced to fully explain it.

Children's saving: A study in the development of economic behaviour takes us literally to the origins of the problem, to childhood, where the lifelong road of acquiring and implementing economic values and concepts begins. It is here that we must begin, in the deep roots of childhood, if the complex nature of saving behaviour among adults is to be fully understood. The answers provided in this book point to many further questions and hypotheses. From an ecological perspective, it is clear that we need to know more about the processes through which economic values and decisions at distal levels come to be understood and implemented in daily proximal interactions. One may ask why there is so little access to economic knowledge. And, what is the function of the discrepancy between the functional values and people's actual saving behaviour?

At the more proximal level, we need to know more, not only about how children perceive their social and economic world, but also about the processes whereby their perceptions and behaviours are shaped. Are children influenced mainly by behaviour that is modelled and incidentally reinforced in the absence of direct teaching of economic strategies? Is the behaviour modelled and reinforced in the same way in all contexts? Is it congruent with economic values? Which contexts and behaviours best promote which values? Only by finding answers to these and other questions will society be enabled to take effective measures to increase its saving, after deciding (as most countries already have) that this is both necessary and appropriate. We look forward to many interesting replications and extensions of Sonuga-Barke and Webley's study in many countries.

9

An Epilogue: Towards an Integral Developmental Economic Psychology

A reply by Edmund J. S. Sonuga-Barke & Paul Webley

INTRODUCTION

In this book we have outlined a way of thinking about the development of children's economic behaviour in Western consumer societies. Our main aim has not been to formulate a particular theory of development, although a theory of the socialisation of saving behaviour is suggested towards the end of the book, but rather to outline a set of metatheoretical assumptions that provide an adequate basis for the study of children's economic development. In many ways this book does not sit so comfortably beside much contemporary Western developmental (meta-) theorising. The book does not present a general theory of human development. Rather our desire was to outline an approach that allows one to address the peculiarly practical issues surrounding the development of economic behaviour. In other words our goal was an integral developmental economic psychology.

After briefly setting out the basis upon which our developmental economic psychology was to be built we went on to describe a number of experimental studies of age related changes in children's saving behaviour. We then attempted to explain these changes using an account of the emergence of saving behaviour that resembles, both in form and function, the ideals of economic practice embedded in Western populist culture. Given the limitations of the experiments we saw the account of development presented as being at best tentative. We felt however that it might provoke comment and provide a basis for future experimental work and theoretical analysis. In this frame of mind we sought and very gratefully received the wide ranging and pithy comments and criticisms from Professor Berti in Chapter 7 and Dr Sharone & Professor Shlomo Maital in Chapter 8.

In this the last chapter we will, in the light of these comments, attempt to draw together the various threads of thought unwound in the main body of the book. Having done this we will, we hope, be able to weave, if not a glorious tapestry, at least a durable rug that will provide the warp and weft upon which a theory of economic development could be fashioned.

Much of the credit, if credit is due, for this final chapter should go to our commentators, Sharone and Shlomo Maital, and Anna Berti. As well as providing two fascinating discussions of the development of economic thought and action, they produced telling analyses of the general principles, experimental studies and theoretical speculation associated with the socio-developmental position. Both commentaries were critical, well informed and contemporary. Our grateful thanks go to all three scholars. Because of their contribution we feel we are in a position to re-present the main themes of the book with increased clarity and cohesion.

We will attempt to do this by taking this opportunity to flesh out certain aspects of the general approach briefly described in the book. We have chosen to concentrate on general principles rather than particular aspects as we feel that our failure to present these principles fully and clearly in the original text may have contributed to some confusion.

Our discussion will focus on the one question that in a sense has provided the central theme of this entire book: Which approach provides the most appropriate basis for an integral or authentic developmental economic psychology? At the heart of our attempt to answer this question will be a re-consideration of the relative merits of two broadly defined positions. Under the broad heading of cognitive developmentalism we will once again pay particular attention to the structuralism of neo-Piagetian approaches. There have, of course, been frequent and varied criticisms of the assumptions underlying this perspective (see Broughton, 1981a; 1981b; 1981c; 1981d; 1981e). In the first part of this chapter we will discuss these criticisms in the light of our reassertion of three principles of our approach to developmental economic psychology. First that the child's economic behaviour should be placed in its proper cultural and historical context. Second that both function and form of the child's economic behaviour should be studied. Third, that function can only be understood from the child's point of view and that any developmental economic psychology must therefore be child- rather than adult-centred.

In Chapter 7 Berti comments on the recent developments made by cognitive approaches to economic development. She talks about the computer metaphor of information processing models and the representationalism of script or schema approaches. Although these approaches differ considerably on the level of particular theory, their contributions to developmental economic psychology are structured by a set of epistemological assumptions that guarantee the primacy of economic thought over action and so tend to dismiss considerations of the functional nature of the economic. This emphasis, we have argued, is the result of a common lack of concern for the meaning of the economic and its history.

The eco-systems approach described by the Maitals in Chapter 8 is, in many ways, similar to the socio-developmental approach. In particular they share a common concern with the role of social and cultural context in the process of human developments.

CONCERNING THE METATHEORETICAL PRINCIPLES OF AN INTEGRAL DEVELOPMENTAL ECONOMIC PSYCHOLOGY

First Principle: Divine the Meaning and Value of Social and Economic Action from its Historical and Cultural Context

A common criticism leveled at neo-Piagetian approaches is that they underestimate the role played by cultural variations in traditions of thought and representations of reality as these influence the process of development as well as our understanding of that process (Broughton, 1981d; Valsiner, 1987). One need only look at the role played by his own philosophical heritage, the Western tradition of thought, in Piaget's developmental theorising to see this very clearly (Fabricius, 1983).

Piaget's programme has been seen as an exercise in epistemology rather than developmental psychology (Brainerd, 1978). At its grandest Piaget's genetic epistemology has been recognised as part of that classical philosophical tradition which has tried to understand the relationship between the relatively stable, structured and permanent nature of ideas or knowledge and the constantly changing sense experience from which they derive. In essence, under the influence of Kant's constructivism, he attempted to marry two European philosophical traditions within a developmental framework; European rationalism and British empiricism are integrated within a structural interpretation of the ascent to reason of both societies as a whole and individual children within modern societies. In this scheme "scientific rationality" in the form of formal operational thought, grows out of the dynamic of assimilation and accommodation that occur as children interact with their physical and social environment.

Jenks (1982) has argued that Piaget presents the abstract hypothetico-deductive reasoning associated with formal operations as both a natural and universally accepted "goal" of cognitive development. He argues that issues of the meaning of competence and maturity in intellectual life are not addressed by

Piaget and the possibility of cultural variations in views about the highest form of reasoning are not entertained. Although critics have identified the cultural heritage that has structured Piaget's values and ideas of truth (Vidal, 1987) he himself played down this influence and at the same time explicitly rejected the integrity of cultural variations in norms of intellectual life and developmental trajectories, tending instead to regard such variations as interpretable only as a stage on the path toward some universal developmental goal (Chapman, 1988).

The influence of this approach on the study of children's economic thought has been considerable. Most importantly it has distracted researchers from thinking about the role played by culture and history in definitions of the "economic". For the most part researchers have tended to regard this meaning as static and "given", so that this research tradition has ignored important aspects of the relationship between this meaning and forms of economic thought, values and actions in contemporary Western society.

In the present book we have tried to address this issue directly. We have based our approach on the assumption that the development of a specifically economic way of thinking and acting can only be understood when clearly situated within the practical world of popular economic culture. This culture in turn needs to be placed in the context of the thoughts and actions of generations of individuals who have drawn and redrawn the boundaries of personal morality, communal responsibility and legitimate individual economic endeavour in Western societies; the history of economic thought (Pribram, 1983).

We have argued that the first stage in the construction of a new developmental economic psychology is to place the meaning of the "economic" within its proper cultural and historical context. The implications of this for developmental economic psychology are clear. Definitions of the "economic" should be coloured by an understanding of the significance of the common language of popular economic culture and informed by an awareness of the values, the definitions of truth and legitimate practical action, that underpin its structures. Only then, do we believe, can the meaning of the term "economic" be understood as it relates to the everyday lives of children.

On one level the values underpinning the idea of the "economic" in Western societies are operationalised in the vocabulary of practical rationality. To say that something is rational in the economic sense is to make reference to commonly held views about the acceptability and legitimacy of economic values and practices. The culture of the "economic" informed by this language thus embodies an idea of the legitimacy of the motives and beliefs underpinning the goals of practical action (McCloskey, 1986).

It is clear from Chapter 5 that there are many ways in which children come into contact with the language of our populist economic culture. This language and the accompanying images must inevitably colour children's economic aspirations.

We suggested that like other vocabularies that adopt a pseudo-moral tone, this vocabulary of economic rationality can be seen to incorporate both prescriptive and descriptive aspects (see Chapter 5). It gives information both about what are the acceptable ends of individual actions and the various strategies for achieving those ends.

Cognitive developmentalists have failed to draw a proper distinction between these two elements of the rhetoric of popular economics. They have highlighted descriptive aspects of this language by concentrating on the child's understanding of the means (institutional or casual), rather than the ends of economic activity. Because of this they have tended to ignore the values and aspirations upon which economic activity in Western societies is based. They define the means as economic without reference to the ends—the goals of this economic activity. But in matters of practical economics, where knowledge of the relationships between agents and institutions subserves the reproduction of social and cultural norms about acceptable action, the means without the ends are as redundant as the ends without the means are frustrating.

Once this truth is agreed it leads to a shift in perspective. We need to look at both the formal and the functional significance of economic thought and action. Behaviours like saving are formal expressions of the system of values that express culture-specific economic ideals and represent more or less approved means of reaching the ends defined by those ideals.

What then are these ideals that have shaped the economic aspirations and determined the particular notion of rational action that operate in Western societies? In Chapter 5 we carried out a brief survey of the history of the "economic" in Western Europe. From that we saw that there is no clearer expression of the relationship between our recent social history and the values underlying an economic model of rational action than that suggested by the phrase "Economic Man" (Lea et al., 1987). On the sociological rather than the formal level of economic analysis, the history of Economic Man is the history of a rational hedonist.

Abercrombie, Hill and Turner (1980) have emphasised the importance of regarding the ascent of the ideal of individualism embodied within Economic Man as a product of historical change. Economic Man is thus a social construction and a period specific expression of what constitutes rational human action. In other words the common aspirations of those in the West are not universal, natural and fixed but are the product of historical definition and redefinition of the boundaries between collective responsibility and the search for individual well-being.

Initially cast as the villain (Machiavelli, 1988/1640) Economic Man was destined to become the hero of Victorian self-help fictions (see Smiles, 1875). Economic historians have highlighted the changes in social outlook that occurred with the spread of Calvinism following the reformation as important factors in the ascent of Economic Man. Weber (1904/1976) suggested that two distinct qualities of the Protestant life contributed to the emergence of the spirit of rationalism associated with Economic Man.

First was the Protestant emphasis on the secular calling (Fullerton, 1928). Protestantism extolled the virtues of hard work in everyday life, which Weber argues, led to diligence in industry and so to the production of capital. Second was the emphasis on thrift made by the Protestant divines. These two factors combined by necessity led to the accumulation of capital. With the rise of secular modernism, Economic Man reached ascendency as a metaphor for this individualistic view of rational action when industry and thrift were directed not to the glory of God but to the glory of human beings. The sacred nature of the productive life was transformed into modern capitalism.

Since the turn of the century this view of the legitimate pursuit of personal well-being as a model of rational action has undergone a process of reification. Social theorists, such as Spencer, Mill, and Bentham and the socio-biologists that followed stressed the instinctive nature of self interest and gave the values associated with self interest a biological rather than an historical significance. Neo-classical economists, for their part, have given this view of human nature a formal expression. This expression of the concept of Economic Man can be seen as the purest expression of the norms associated with an individualistic means-end rationality. Indeed Boulding (1969) has stressed the importance of the role that economists have played in the socio-historical process of defining the meaning and popular usage of the term economic. In many ways this process of reification is continued by many developmental psychologists who eschew issues of the meaning and legitimacy of economic action and who view the appearance of certain forms of economic thought and action during development as unproblematic (Buck-Morse, 1975).

But the emergence of the saving ethic and the view that saving was an essential aspect of "economic hygiene" and civilised conduct can also be tied to particular historical periods (Maital & Maital, Chapter 8, this volume; see Smiles, 1875). With the rise of the Protestant ethic in and around the time of the reformation, the perennial spiritual virtues of "patience" and "forbearance" were translated into the economic virtue of "thrift". Words that had for centuries encapsulated the Christian message of spiritual fortitude were given a secular significance and were used to regulate the economic, rather than the spiritual, affairs of people. To be thrifty is to wait for more valued rewards available in the future, even when less valued rewards are available in the present.

To recap, the "culture of the economic" as it exists in Western societies is founded on a tradition of thought defined in terms of a particular theory of practical rationality within which both the form and the function of economic thought and activity are grounded. When this is recognised, we automatically return to the "economic" its functional significance. In the case of the practical affairs of the "economic" the isolation from cultural meaning and rejection of functional significance go hand in hand.

At this point it might be helpful to reflect on two interesting issues raised by our commentators in Chapters 7 and 8.

Reflections on the Role of Culture in Development.   The first reflection is on the role of cultural context in the development of children's economic behaviour. This is prompted by Berti's doubts about our account of the possible role of non-functional economic behaviour, encouraged by parents, in the eventual development of functional economic behaviour.

The first observation that should be made is that it is inevitable that a particular theory of economic development based on broad socio-developmental principles will emphasise the importance of social and cultural factors in development. It will look to those social institutions, family, friends and media, that are likely to play an important role in the child's "apprentice-ship" in economic thought and action (Rogoff, 1990). In recent years there has been an increasingly clear appreciation of the role played by social context in the emergence of particular ways of thinking. The idea that abstract and formal scientific ways of thinking about the world emerge "naturally" has given way to the view that these approaches are actively encouraged by educational technologies tailored to the practical requirements of each culture.

This new approach is summed up by Rogoff (1990, p.6) who writes that:

> A broader view of cognition and context requires that the task characteristics and cognitive performance be considered in the light of the goal of activity and its interpersonal and socio-cultural context. The purpose of thinking is to act effectively; activities are goal directed (tacitly or implicitly) with social and cultural definition of goals and means of handling problems.

The imperialism of the Piagetian formulation of formal thought as the fundamental developmental goal has been overturned and replaced by a view of the ideologically based nature of conceptions of rational thought and action (Goodnow, 1980). Consequently Western developmental psychologists have been more and more willing to attribute an important role to social (Doise & Mackie, 1981; Light and Glachan, 1985) and cultural factors (Goodnow, 1990) in the process of cognitive development. The influence of these factors is recognised both in terms of defining what are legitimate ways of thinking as well as in the way social contact can facilitate acquisition of the "right" ways of thinking.

Of course many vehicles for this process of social influence on the development of thought have been suggested (Bruner, 1983; Doise, 1985; Trevarthen, 1988; Vygotsky, 1987). We speculated that the young child's actual early economic practice might play an important role in the development of more sophisticated expressions of Western economic identity later on. We argued that social institutions encourage a savings habit in young children.

Despite the fact that saving at this age is not based on a functional understanding, it does provide the children with the repeated opportunity to evaluate the economic and social value of saving. This experience, then, can be seen as providing the basis for a functional understanding of saving as parents show their children that saving money is an acceptable and effective way of solving the problems presented under income constraint. We also argued that this shift from non-functional to functional economic behaviour is accompanied by a change in the way that value is assigned to "economic" actions. Young children see the value of an action as defined in primarily social terms and older children see it as being defined in primarily economic terms. This shift in perspective is most clearly seen in Study 3.

We are very grateful to Berti for her comments on our speculations about the relationship between functional and non-functional aspects of saving during development. We would however argue that by stressing the development of economic competence through practice guided by social institutions we have presented a useful way of characterising the data from the range of studies reported. Berti outlines two separate problems with our account. First she argues that there is in fact little evidence that a period of non-functional saving exists.

We would argue that from an empirical point of view that there is little doubt that 6 year old children in our study did not understand the economic function of saving, and that by the age of 12 they did. We do however concede that the question of whether or not this stage is accompanied by the establishment of a savings "habit" depended on the context within which the behaviour was studied. What is clear is that nearly all the 6 year olds studied did save in real life (in one way or another) and that none of them understood the economic functions of saving. Whether or not the saving behaviour of the 6 year olds could rightly be described as a habit, it seems fairly safe to speculate that this non-functional saving would provide an ideal context for the effective socialisation of a more reasoned and pragmatic approach to money management.

Berti also argues that there is very little evidence that parents and the media are actively involved in the inculcation of a savings habit. At this point it needs to be emphasised how little socialisation involves explicit and didactic attempts to teach culturally acceptable behaviour, their value and function.

We have in fact argued that this is not the level at which saving is socialised. We have concentrated on the role of parents and banks in the rewarding of a savings habit that we have argued provides the basis for a functional understanding later on in development. While Berti is right that neither the parents nor the banks laid a great emphasis on the functional or categorical value of saving, they did attempt, from a position of power, to encourage a savings habit in their children, very often by rewarding the accumulation of savings—an economic practice upon which ideas of the instrumental and pseudo-moral aspects of the language of saving could then be established.

Despite Berti's criticisms we still see the account of the development of effective economic practice as a useful alternative to presently existing structural accounts of development.

Reflections on Economic Education and "Civilisation".   The second reflection is on the potential role of formal education in the principles and practice of economics. In Chapter 7 the Maital's call for intervention in the process of economic socialisation. We would like to counsel caution. The problem as we see it is that before you educate children in the principles of economics you must first decide which system of economics you wish to teach. How would you as a teacher decide between the principles of Capitalist, Marxist or for that matter Islamic economics? Certainly, it should not be too difficult to explain the principles upon which each of these economic systems is based, and the attitudes to say profit, saving and interest encouraged by each. The issue becomes more complicated when you take your mandate to teach economics as an invitation to assert in a positive manner a particular form of economic practice. This seems to be what the Maital's are calling for when they ask for intervention in economic *socialisation.*

Although some might see the development of modernist economics as the foundation of a "developed civilised society" others would not. The whole issue of thrift and personal saving is particularly interesting in this respect. Should children be taught to save? Whereas self control and moral fortitude have been universally and perennially recognised as the basis of a virtuous life, the acceptance of the idea that these concepts have meaning and value when translated from a spiritual onto a purely material plane is limited to certain societies during certain periods of history.

In fact, religious traditions are unanimous in their advice against placing too much emphasis on the provision of future well-being. Although many reading this book will be familiar with Christ's call in the Sermon on the Mount to "take therefore no thought of tomorrow" (Matthew, 6; 34) it is less likely that you will be familiar with the Quaranic verse in the *Sura Maaa-'idah* warning of the dangers of the accumulation of savings. This mistrust of an emphasis is not restricted to Semitic forms. For instance, the Hindu master Vasishtha's advice in the Ramayana to his pupil Prince Rama "to fix [his] attention upon the present moment, and not to employ [his] thoughts on the past or the future" is irreconcilable with the thrift ethic so strongly advocated in the self-help philosophy of Protestant social theorists.

While the significance of these traditional teachings will not be agreed by all, we mention them simply to reinforce the point that what to (some) Westerners seem to be the very foundations upon which a successful society is built, may seem wholly subversive when seen in the light of the teachings of other traditions.

Moving on from this it could be argued that any attempt to educate children in one particular set of principles of economic practice is to actively partake in the process of reification of economic practices that are really only embodiments of a set of historically situated culturally determined set of values. From a Marxist point of view such a process of education could be seen as an exercise in class domination and from an Islamic point of view contemporary Western imperialism.

Our book presents an analysis of the development of a behaviour—saving—that has a historically determined meaning and a conditional value. This book is not a positive call to intervention. It is debatable whether saving is or is not sensible or moral. The analysis presented in this book does not and cannot contribute to that debate.

Second Principle: Move from Contextual Analysis to a Functional Analysis

The cognitive approach to development has also been criticised by many for the way in which it has limited its agenda to the study of the attainment of abstract knowledge and the emergence of reasoned thought at the expense of other forms of knowledge and modes of thought (cf. Gilligan, 1982).

From what we have already written in this chapter we can see that the history of the "economic" is a practical history of the acquisition, management and distribution of scarce resources. The culture of the economic is a practical culture, not populated by "Epistemological Man", who is called to knowledge, but rather by "Economic Man" who is called to acquisition. It is this emphasis on the functions of "economic" actions and their relationship to the actions of other economic agents and institutions that differentiates what might be called developmental economic psychology from other developmental social psychologies.

As we have suggested, from this point of view it becomes clear that the specifically economic meaning of these agents and institutions is apparent only when their functional as well as their formal significance is recognised. Because of a failure to recognise this, neo-Piagetian approaches have tended to adopt a purely nominal definition of the economic. The term economic has simply served as a label for the subset of categories and concepts associated with the "social" world of economics.

As we have suggested, this failure to appreciate the need for a functional analysis stems from the fact that cognitive developmentalists make no attempt at a serious analysis of the nature of economic action—in terms of its historical or cultural basis.

Once again this emphasis of function is in line with recent general accounts of cognitive development. The concern for function, it seems to us, is an inevitable consequence of the desire, already discussed, of developmental psychologists to situate the actions and cognitions of children within particular contexts. This close relationship between functional and contextual analysis is nicely expressed in the passage from Rogoff (1990) quoted earlier. Once cognition is situated in time and space its particular functions become apparent.

Reflections on Function, Context and the Development of Economic Thought.   At this point it might be helpful to dwell on the functionalist and contextualist credentials of the socio-developmental position. There seems to be a difference of opinion over the "world view" that our book incorporates. Berti in her commentary describes it as incorporating a "traditional view of behaviourism". It is true that the approach taken is not cognitivist. At no point do we feel the need to drop to the level of hypothetical mental structures for an explanation of development. However we are of course very interested in cognitions of various kinds. The issues surrounding children's thinking about the value of actions, their attitudes to saving, their adoption and articulation of strategies and the historical development of ideologies and the social transmission of representations are all themes that are discussed in this book. The notion that this culture of ideas, linguistic and non-linguistic, provides a context for the development of particular values and the practical and social means of attaining them is at the very heart of the analysis presented in this book. Rather than being behaviourist in any traditional sense our approach is contextualist and functionalist. We assert the need to base any analysis and explanation of development within its proper cultural and historical context. From the socio-developmental point of view certain ends are defined as valuable and certain means as functional. Like behaviourists we are interested in the instrumental nature of actions, but unlike (most) behaviourists we argue that instrumentality is conditional on ideas about value and function held within a community and passed down to or constructed by children. The idea that the economic behaviour of children is a series of responses maintained *directly* by the environment (either social or physical) is no part of our approach at all. The relationship between the child and the material world of goods is mediated by representations of the legitimacy of action derived from social agents and institutions.

Furthermore our criticism of the traditional approach to the study of economic development is not that it has ignored behaviour *per se*, but rather that because it has ignored behaviour it has failed to recognise the inherently functional nature of the "economic" generally and saving in particular. For instance, the types of questions typically posed by researchers working in the cognitive developmentalist tradition have tended to be impersonal and non functional in nature. The difference between these questions and those asked in our study is nicely highlighted in Berti's chapter in the section on children's conceptions of banking. The questions about the bank did not ask about "the usefulness" of banks and "focused on the world of adults" (Chapter 7). We would argue that the relevance of these sorts of questions to the study of the actual development of children's economic thought and behaviour is highly questionable. This takes us nicely onto the third principle upon which an integral developmental economic psychology should be based.

Third Principle; Take the Child's Point of View

The main practical implication of this functional approach is that it encourages us to centre on the children's own understanding of their economic world and the problems presented in it. This involves the recognition that the status of the individual as an economic actor is defined in terms of their response to problems of resource allocation, rather than just in terms of their knowledge about the working of the formal world of grown-up economic systems. This is because on one level, an understanding of functions typically ascribed by adults to actions and institutions becomes irrelevant when one attempts to explain the way children actually act and think, and to understand the developmental significance of those actions and thoughts. Because the traditional neo-Piagetian approach has concentrated on formal aspects of economic life it has tended to see the child as in some way apart from adult economic culture, acting on that culture but not directly involved in it. In other words it has adopted an adult centred view of economic development. The world of economics is seen as something out there, about which children acquire knowledge as they grow.

But the child is an integral part of that culture. More specifically children inhabit an economic subculture all of their own; a subculture that is dependent, both culturally and materially, on, but separate from, that of the adult. What we mean by this is that the growing child is faced with, and has to solve problems of practical importance in their own life. The economic world of the child is a world full of practical problems, that have significance for the child in their own right and almost certainly as a training ground in providing solutions to the economic problems of the world of grown-ups (Webley & Webley, 1990).

The approaches taken by children and adults to solving these problems may be different and be given different names. Whereas young children may save in a piggy bank, bet, and swap, adults may have a multi-service bank account, speculate, and deal and trade—clearly these activities are in many ways functionally equivalent. Because of their reliance on Piagetian approaches the practical economic world of the child has been almost completely ignored by traditional studies of economic development.

This implies that although the strategies found within the formal world of adult economics provide effective means to solve these sorts of economic problems, these formal institutions do not need to exist in order for economic action to occur.

IN SUMMARY

We believe that these three principles provide an appropriate basis for the development of an integral development psychology. Let us recap while at the same time turning the order in which we presented these principles on its head. First, we can say that only when one takes the child's point of view, the meanings and values that they ascribe to actions, can one understand the functional nature of those actions. Only once the functions of those actions are situated within the cultural web of the value system of Western popular economics, does their full significance as particular embodiments of those values become apparent.

References

Abercrombie, N., Hill, S., & Turner, T. (1980). *The dominant ideology thesis.* Harmondsworth: Allen Lane.

Abercrombie, N., Hill, S., & Turner, T. (1986). *Sovereign individuals of capitalism.* Harmondsworth: Allen Lane.

Ainslie, G. A. (1975). Impulse control in pigeons. *Journal of the Experimental Analysis of Behavior, 21,* 485–498.

Ainslie, G. A. (1984). Behavorial economics II: Motivated, involuntary behavior. *Social Science information, 23.*

Ainslie, G. A., & Hernnstien, R. J. (1981). Preference reversal and delayed reinforcement. *Animal Learning & Behavior, 9,* 476–482.

Ajello, A. M., & Bombi, A. S. (1988). *Studi sociali e conoscenze economiche. Un curricolo per la scuola elementare.* Florence: La Muova Italia.

Ajello, A. M., Bombi, A. S., Pontecorvo, C., & Zucchermaglio, C. (1986). Understanding agriculture as an economic activity: The role of figurative information. *European Journal of Psychology of Education, 41,* 295–306.

Ajello, A. M., Bombi, A. S., Pontecorvo, C., & Zucchermaglio, C. (1987). Teaching economics in the primary school: The concepts of work and profit. *International Journal of Behavioral Development, 10,* 51–69.

Antonides, G. (1990, November). *Psychological factors in the lifetimes of a durable good.* Paper presented to the Royal Netherlands Academy colloquium on "The timing of consumption and the consumption of time", Amsterdam.

Aponte, H. J., & VanDeusen, J. M. (1981). Structural family therapy. In A. S. Gurman, & D. P. Kniskern (Eds.), *Handbook of family therapy.* New York: Brunner/Mazel.

Bandura, A. (1982). Self-efficacy mechanism in human agency. *American Psychologist,* February, 122–147.

Bandura, A. (1989). Human agency in social cognitive theory. *American Psychologist,* September, 1175–1184.

Baxter, E. H. (1976). Children's and adolescent's perceptions of occupational prestige. *Canadian Review of Sociology & Anthropology, 13*, 229–238.

Berti, A. E. (in press). Capitalism and socialism: How 7th graders understand and misunderstand the information presented in their geography textbooks. *European Journal of Psychology of Education.*

Berti, A. E., & Bombi, A. S. (1981). The development of the concept of money and its value: A developmental study. *Child Development, 52*, 1179–82.

Berti, A. E., & Bombi, A. S. (1988). *The child's construction of economics.* Cambridge, UK: Cambridge University Press.

Berti, A. E., Bombi, A. S., & De Beni, R. (1986a). Acquiring economic notions: Profit. *International Journal of Behavioral Development, 9*, 15–29.

Berti, A. E., Bombi, A. S., & De Beni, R. (1986b). The development of economic notions: Single sequence or separate acquisition? *Journal of Economic Psychology, 7*, 415–424.

Berti, A. E., Bombi, A. S., & Lis, A. (1982). The child's conceptions about means of productions and their owners. *European Journal of Social Psychology, 12*, 221–239.

Berti, A. E., & De Beni, R. (1988). Prerequisites for the concept of profit: Logic and memory. *British Journal of Developmental Psychology, 16*, 361–368.

Berti, A. E., & Grivet, A. (1990). The development of economic reasoning in children from 8 to 13 years old: Price mechanism. *Contributi dei Dipartimenti e degli Istituti Italiani di Psicologia.*

Boehm-Bewark, E. von (1891). *Capital and interest* (Trans. W. Smart). New York: Strechert.

Bolger, N., Caspi, G., Downey, G., & Moorehouse, M. (1988) Development in context: Research perspectives. In N. Bolger, A. Caspi, G. Downey, & M. Moorehouse (Eds.), *Persons in context: Developmental processes.* Cambridge, UK: Cambridge University Press.

Boulding, K. (1969). Economics as a moral science. *American Economic Review, 59*, 1–12.

Boyle, P., & Murray, J. (1979). Social security wealth and private saving in Canada. *Canadian Journal of Economics, 12*, 456–467.

Brainerd, C. J. (1978). *Piaget's theory of intelligence.* Englewood Cliffs, NJ: Prentice Hall.

Brim, O. (1966). Socialization through the life cycle. In O. Brim & S. Wheelers (Eds.), *Socialization after childhood: Two essays.* New York: Wiley.

Bronfenbrenner, U. (1986). Ecology of the family as a context for human development: Research perspectives. *Developmental Psychology, 22*, 723–742.

Bronfenbrenner, U. (1988a). Interacting systems in human development. Research paradigms: present and future. In N. Bolger, A. Caspi, G. Downey, & M. Moorehouse. (Eds.), *Persons in context: Developmental processes.* Cambridge, UK: Cambridge University Press.

Bronfenbrenner, U. (1988b). Foreword. In A. R. Pence, (Ed.), *Ecological research with children and families: From concepts to methodology.* New York: Teacher's College, Columbia University.

Bronfenbrenner, U. (1989). Ecological systems theory. *Annals of Child Development, 6*, 187–249.

Bronfenbrenner, U., & Crouter, A. C. (1983). The evolution of environmental models in developmental research. In W. I. Kessen (Ed.), P. H. Mussen (Series Ed.), *Handbook of child Psychology: Vol. 1. History, theory, and methods.* New York: Wiley.

Broughton, J. M. (1981a). Piaget's structural developmental psychology I; Piaget and structuralism. *Human Development, 24*, 78–109.

Broughton, J. M. (1981b). Piaget's structural developmental psychology II; Logic and psychology. *Human Development, 24*, 195–224.

Broughton, J. M. (1981c). Piaget's structural developmental psychology III; Function and the problem of knowledge. *Human Development, 24*, 257–285.

Broughton, J. M. (1981d). Piaget's structural developmental psychology IV; knowledge without self and without history. *Human Development, 24*, 320–346.

Broughton, J. M. (1981e). Piaget's structural developmental psychology V; Ideology-critique and the possibility of a critical developmental psychology. *Human Development, 24*, 382–411.

Brown, A. L., & Barclay, C. R. (1976). The effects of training specific mnemonics on the metamnemonic efficiency of retarded children. *Child Development, 47,* 71–80.

Bruner, J. (1983). *Child's talk: Learning to use language.* New York: Norton.

Buck-Morse, J. (1975). Socio-economic bias in Piaget's theory and its implications for cross cultural studies. *Human Development, 18,* 35–49.

Burris, V. L. (1983). Stages in the development of economic concepts. *Human Relations, 36,* 791–812.

Carey, S. (1985). *Conceptual change in childhood.* Cambridge, MA: MIT Press.

Carroll, C., & Summers, L. (1989). *Consumption growth parallels income growth: Some new evidence.* Harvard University: Economics Department, working paper.

Case, R. (1985). *Intellectual development. Birth to adulthood.* New York: Academic Press.

Chapman, M. (1988). Contextuality and directionality of cognitive development. *Human Development, 31,* 92–106.

Claar, A. (1987, August). *The development of economic understanding in adolescence: The concept of money.* Paper presented to the Fourth International Conference on "Event Perception and Action", Trieste, Italy.

Clower, R. W., & Johnson, M. B. (1968). Income, wealth and the theory of consumption. In N. Wolfe (Ed.), *Value, capital & growth.* Edinburgh: Edinburgh University Press.

Cochran, M., Larner, M., Riley, D., Gunnarsson, L., & Henderson, C. R. Jr. (1990). *Extending families: The social networks of parents and their children.* Cambridge, UK: Cambridge University Press.

Confrey, J. (1990). A review of research on students' conceptions in mathematics, science, and programming. In C. B. Cazden (Ed.), *Review of research in education.* Washington DC: American Educational Research Association.

Connell, R. W. (1977). *Ruling class, ruling culture.* Melbourne: Cambridge University Press.

Cordes, J. J., Galper, H., & Kirby, S. N. (1990). *Causes of overwithholding: Forced saving transactions cost?* George Washington University, Economics Department, working paper.

Courant, P., Gramlich, E., & Laitner, J. (1986). A dynamic micro estimate of the life cycle model. In H. J. Aaron, & G. Burtless (Eds.), *Retirement and economic behaviour.* Washington, DC: Brookings Institution.

Cram, F., & Ng, S. H. (1989). Children's endorsement of ownership attribute. *Journal of Economic Psychology, 10,* 63–75.

Damon, W. (1977). *The social world of the child.* San Francisco: Jossey-Bass Publishers.

Dannefer, D., & Perlmutter, M. (1990). Development as a multidimensional process: Individual and social constituents. *Human Development, 33,* 108–137,

Danziger, K. (1958). Children's earliest conceptions of economic relationships (Australia). *Journal of Genetic Psychology, 91,* 231–240.

Dickins, D., & Ferguson, V. (1957). *Practices and attitudes of rural white children concerning money.* (Technical report No. 43) MS. Mississippi State College, Agricultural Experimental Station.

Doise, W. (1985). Social regulation in cognitive development. In R. A. Hinde, A. N. Perret-Clermont, & J. Stevenson-Hinde (Eds.), *Social relationships and cognitive development.* Oxford: Clarendon Press.

Doise, W., & Mackie, D. (1981). On the social nature of cognition. In J. P. Forgas (Ed.), *Social cognition: Perspectives on everyday understanding.* London: Academic Press.

Duhl, B. S., & Duhl, F. J. (1981). Integrative family therapy. In A. S. Gurman & D. P. Kniskerneds (Eds.), *Handbook of family therapy.* New York: Brunner/Mazel.

Echeita, G. (1985). *El mundo adulto en la mente de los niños. La compresion infantil de las relaciones de intercambio y el efecto de la interaction social sobre su desarrollo.* Unpublished manuscript.

Emler, N., & Dickinson, J. (1985). Children's representations of economic inequality. *British Journal of Developmental Psychology, 3,* 191–198.

Fabricius, W. V. (1983). Piaget's theory of knowledge: its philosophical context. *Human Development, 26*, 325–334.

Fabricius, W. V., & Wellman, H. M. (1984) Memory development. *Journal of Children in Contemporary Society, 16*, 171–187.

Ferenczi, S. (1914/1976). The ontogenesis of the interest in money. In E. Bornemann (Ed.), *The psychoanalysis of money*. New York: Urizen.

Ferguson, C. E., & Gould, J. P. (1975). *Micro-economic theory*. Homeswood, IL: Richard Irwin.

Fisher, I. (1930). *The theory of interest*. New York: Macmillan.

Fisher, K. W. (1980). A theory of cognitive development: The control and construction of hierarchies of skills. *Psychological Review, 87*, 447–531.

Flavell, J. H. (1971). Stage related properties of cognitive development. *Cognitive Psychology, 2*, 421–453.

Flavell, J. H., & Wellman, H. M. (1977). Metamemory. In R. V. Kail Jr. & J. W. Hagen. (Eds.), *Perspectives on the development of memory and cognition*. Hillsdale, NJ: Lawrence Erlbaum Associates Inc.

Flavell, J. H., & Wholwill, J. F. (1969). Formal and functional aspects of cognitive development. In D. Elkind & J. H. Flavell (Eds.), *Essays in honour of Jean Piaget*. London: Oxford University Press.

Fox, K. (1978). What children bring to school: The beginnings of economic education. *Social Education, 10*, 478–481.

Freire, E., Gorman, B., & Wessman, A. E. (1980). Temporal span, delay of gratification and children's socio-economic status. *Journal of Genetic Psychology, 137*, 247–255.

Freud, S. (1908/1959). Character and anal eroticism. In J. Strachey (Ed.), *The standard edition of complete psychological works of Freud*. (Vol. 9). London: Hogarth.

Freud, S. (1911). *Formulations of the two principles of mental functioning*. Penguin Freud Library (Vol II). Middlesex: Penguin.

Friedman, M. (1953). *Essays in positive economics*. Chicago: University of Chicago Press.

Friedman, M. (1957). *A theory of consumption function*. Princeton. NJ: Princeton University Press.

Fullerton, K. (1928). Calvinism and capitalism. *The Harvard Theological Review*, 163–191.

Furnham, A. (1986). Children's understanding of the economic world. *Australian Journal of Education, 30*, 219–240.

Furnham, A., & Cleare, A. (1988). School children's conceptions of economics: Prices, wages, investments and strikes. *Journal of Economic Psychology, 9*, 467–479.

Furnham, A., & Thomas, P. (1984). Pocket money: A study of economic education. *British Journal of Developmental Psychology, 2*, 205–212.

Furth, H. G. (1970). *Piaget for teachers*. Englewood Cliffs, NJ: Prentice Hall.

Furth, H.G. (1980). *The world of grown-ups*. New York: Elsevier.

Furth, H. G., Baur, M., & Smith, J. E. (1976). Children's conceptions of social institutions: A Piagetian framework. *Human Development, 19*, 351–374.

Galin, M. (1989). *Economic socialization of Israeli Youths*. Unpublished M.A. Thesis, Ben Gurion University: Beersheva, Israel.

Gelman, R. (1978). Cognitive Development. *Annual Review of Psychology, 29*, 297–332.

Gilligan, C. F. (1982). *In a different voice*. Cambridge, MA: Harvard University Press.

Goldstein, B., & Oldham, J. (1979). *Children and work: a study of socialization*. New Brunswick: Transaction Press.

Goodnow, J. J. (1980). Everyday concepts of intelligence and its development. In N. Warren (Ed.), *Studies in cross cultural psychology* (Vol. 2). London: Academic Press.

Goodnow, J. J. (1988). Children, families and communities: Ways of viewing their relationships to each other. In N. Bolger, A. Caspi, G. Downey, & M. Moorehouse (Eds.), *Persons in context: Developmental processes*. Cambridge, UK: Cambridge University Press.

Goodnow, J. J. (1990). The socialization of cognition: What's involved? In J. W. Stigler, R. A. Shweder, & G. Herdt. (Eds.), *Cultural psychology: essays on comparative human development.* Cambridge, UK: Cambridge University Press.

Gottlieb, G. (1991). Experiential canalization of behavioral development: Theory. *Developmental Psychology, 27*, 4–13.

Hausman, J., (1979). Individual discount rates and the purchase and utilization of energy-using durables. *Bell Journal of Economics*, Spring.

Horowitz, F. D. (1987). *Exploring developmental theories: Toward a structural/behavioral model of development.* Hillsdale, NJ: Lawrence Erlbaum Associates Inc.

Hussein, G. (1981). *Aspects of school children's understanding of money.* Unpublished manuscript, Exeter University.

Immerwahr, J. (1989). *Saving: Good or Bad?* Public Agenda Foundation, pilot study, New York.

Jahoda, G. (1979). The construction of economic reality by some Glaswegian children. *European Journal of Social Psychology, 9,* 115–127.

Jahoda, G. (1981). The development of thinking about economic institutions: The bank. *Cahiers de Psychologie Cognitive, 1,* 55–73.

Jahoda, G. (1983). European "lag" in the development of an economic concept: A study in Zimbabwe. *British Journal of Developmental Psychology, 1,* 113–120.

Jahoda, G. (1984). The development of thinking about socio-economic systems. In H. Tajfel (Ed.), *The social dimension.* Cambridge: Cambridge University Press.

Jahoda, G., & Woerdenbagch, A. (1982). The development of ideas about an economic institution: a cross-national replication. *British Journal of Social Psychology, 21,* 337–338.

Jenks, C. (1982). Constituting the child. In C. Jenks (Ed.), *The sociology of childhood.* London: Batsford Academic.

Kail, R. (1979). *The development of memory in children.* San Francisco: W. H. Freeman & Co.

Katona, G. (1975). *Psychological economics.* New York: Elsevier.

Kennedy, B. A., & Miller, D. J. (1976). Persistent use of verbal regulation as a function of information about its value. *Child Development, 47,* 566–569.

Kessen, W. (1979). The American Child and other cultural inventions. *American Psychologist, 34,* 815–820.

Keynes, J. M. (1933). *Economic possibilities for our grandchildren: Essays in Persuasion.* London: Macmillan.

Keynes, J. M. (1936). *The general theory of employment, interest and money.* London: Macmillan.

Kohlberg, L. (1976). Moral stages and moralization: The cognitive-developmental approach to socialization. In T. Lickona (Ed.), *Moral development and behavior.* New York: Holt, Rinehart & Winston.

Koskela, E., & Viren, M. (1983). Social security and household saving in an international cross section. *American Economic Review, 73,* 212–217.

Kotlikoff, L., & Summers, L. H. (1981). The role of intergenerational transfers in aggregate capital formation. *Journal of Political Economy, 89,* 706–732.

Kourilsky, M. (1977). The Kinder-Economy: A case study of kindergarten pupils' acquisition of economic concepts. *Elementary School Journal, 77,* 182–191.

Kurz, M., Spiegelman, R. G., & West, R. W. (1973). *The experimental horizon and the role of time preference for the Seattle–Denver income maintenance experiments.* Stanford: Stanford Research Institute, Memorandum No. 21.

La Fontaine, J. de. (1974). *Fables (Livres 1 a VII)* (Originally published 1668–1679). Paris: Gallimard.

Laboratory of Comparative Human Cognition (1983). Culture and cognitive development. In W. I. Kessen (Ed.), P. H. Mussen (Series Ed.), *Handbook of child psychology: Vol. 1. History, theory and methods* (pp.295–356). New York: Wiley.

Lancaster, K. J. (1966). A new approach to consumer theory. *Journal of Political Economy, 74,* 132–157.

Lea, S. E. G., Tarpy, R., & Webley, P. (1987). *The individual in the economy: A survey of economic psychology.* Cambridge, UK: Cambridge University Press.

Leahy, R. L. (1981). The development of the conception of economic inequality: Descriptions and comparisons of rich and poor people. *Child Development, 52,* 523–532.

Leiser, D. (1983). Children's conceptions of economics: The constitution of a cognitive domain. *Journal of Economic Psychology, 4,* 297–317.

Leiser, D., Sevon, G., & Levy, D. (1990). Children's economic socialization: Summarizing the cross-cultural comparisons of ten countries. *Journal of Economic Psychology, 11,* (4).

Lerner, R. M. (1991). Changing organism-context relations as the basic process of development: A development contextual perspective. *Developmental Psychology, 27,* 27–32.

Lerner, R. M., & Kauffman, M. B. (1985). The concept of development in contextualism. *Developmental Review, 5,* 309–333.

Light, P. H., & Glachan, M. (1985). Facilitation of individual problem solving through peer interaction. *Education Psychology, 5,* 217–225.

Light, P. H., & Perret-Clermont, A. N. (1989). Social context effects in learning and testing. In A. Gellatly, D. Rogers, & J. Slaboda (Eds.), *Cognition and social worlds.* Oxford: Clarendon Press.

Logue, A. W. (1988). Research in self control: an integrating framework. *Behavioral & Brain Sciences, 11,* 665–709.

Long, F., Peters, D. L., & Garduque, L. (1985). Continuity between home and day care: A model for defining relevant dimensions of child care. *Advances in Applied Developmental Psychology, 1,* 131–170.

Machiavelli (1988). *The prince.* (First published in Britain 1640). Middlesex: Penguin.

Maital, S. (1982). *Minds, markets and money.* New York: Basic Books.

Maital, S. (1986). Prometheus Rebound: On welfare-improving constraints. *Eastern Economic Journal, XII (3),* 337–344.

Maital, S., & Maital, S. L. (1978). Time preference, delay of gratification and the intergenerational transmission of economic inequality. In O. Ashenfelter & W. Oates (Eds.), *Essays in Labor market analysis.* New York: Wiley.

Maital, S., & Maital, S. L. (1984). *Economic games people play* New York: Basic Books.

Maital, S., Maital, S. L., & Pollak, N. (1986). Economic behavior and social learning theory. In A. Mcfadyen & H. Mcfadyen (Eds.), *Economic psychology.* Amsterdam: North Holland/Elsevier.

Marshall, A. (1890). *Principles of economics* (8th ed., 1962). London: Macmillan.

Marshall, H., & Magruder, L. (1960). Relations between parents' money education practices and children's knowledge and use of money. *Child Development, 31,* 253–284.

McCloskey, D. N. (1986). *The rhetoric of economics.* Brighton, UK: Harvester Wheatsheaf.

McCloskey, M. (1983). Naive theories of motion. In D. Gentner & A. L. Stevens (Eds.), *Mental Models.* Hillsdale, NJ: Lawrence Erlbaum Associates Inc.

McGuinness, T., & Cowling, K. (1975). Advertising and the aggregate demand for cigarettes. *European Economic Review, 6,* 311–328.

Miller, L., & Horn, T. (1955). Children's conceptions regarding debt. *Elementary School Journal, 56,* 209–221.

Miller, P. H., & Bigi, L. (1977). Children's understanding of how stimulus dimensions affect performance. *Child Development, 48,* 1712–1715.

Minuchin, S. (1974). *Families and family therapy.* Cambridge, MA: Harvard University Press.

Minuchin, P. (1985). Families and individual development: Provocation from the field of family therapy. *Child Development, 56,* 289–302.

Mischel, H., & Mischel, W. (1983). The development of children's knowledge of self control strategies. *Child Development, 54,* 603–619.

Mischel, W. (1958). Preference for delayed reward: An experimental study of cultural observation. *Journal of Abnormal & Social Psychology*, *56*, 57–61.

Mischel, W. (1966). Theory and research on the antecedents of self-imposed delay of rewards. In B. A. Maher (Ed.), *Progress in experimental personality research*. New York: Academic Press.

Mischel, W. (1981). Metacognition and delay of gratification. In J. H. Flavell, & L. Ross (Eds.), *Social cognitive development; frontiers and possible futures*. Cambridge, UK: Cambridge University Press.

Mischel, W. (1984). Convergences and challenges in the search for consistency. *American Psychologist*, April, 351–364.

Mischel, W., Ebbensen, E., & Ziess, A. R. (1972) Cognitive and attentional mechanisms in delay of gratification. *Journal of Personality & Social Psychology*, *21*, 204–218.

Mischel, W., & Metzner, R. (1962). Preference for delayed reward as a function of age, intelligence, and length of delay interval. *Journal of Abnormal & Social Psychology*, *64*, 425–431.

Moscovici, S. (1984). The phenomenon of social representations. In R. M. Farr (Ed.), *Social representations*. Cambridge, UK: Cambridge University Press.

Newson, J., & Newson, E. (1976). *Seven years old in the home environment*. London: Allen & Unwin.

Nelson, K. (1986). *Event knowledge*, Hillsdale, NJ: Lawrence Erlbaum Associates Inc.

Ng, S. H. (1983). Children's ideas about the bank and shop profit: Developmental stages and influences of cognitive contrast and conflict. *Journal of Economic Psychology*, *4*, 209–21.

Ng, S. H. (1985). Children's ideas about the bank: A New Zealand replication. *European Journal of Social Psychology*, *15*, 121–123.

Pence, A. R. (1988). *Ecological research with children and families: From concepts to methodology*. New York: Teachers College, Columbia University.

Piaget, J. (1923). *Le langage et la pensée chez l'enfant*. Neuchatel: Delachaux et Niestle.

Piaget, J. (1924). *Le jugement et le raisonnement chez l'enfant*. Neuchatel: Delachaux et Niestle.

Piaget, J. (1925). Psychologie et critique de la connaissance. *Archives de Psychologie*, *19*, 193–210.

Piaget, J. (1926). *La représentation du monde chez l'enfant*. Paris: Alcan.

Piaget, J. (1932). *Le jugement moral chez l'enfant*. Paris: Alcan.

Piaget, J. (1950). *Introduction d l'epistemologie génétique*. Paris: P.U.F.

Piaget, J. (1969). *The child's conception of time*. New York: Baltimore.

Piaget, J. (1970a). *Genetic epistemology*. New York: Columbia University Press.

Piaget, J. (1970b). *The child's conception of movement and speed*. New York: Baltimore.

Pressley, M. (1979). Increasing children's self control through cognitive interventions. *Review of Educational Research*, *49*, 319–370.

Pribram, K. (1983). *A history of economic reasoning*. Baltimore: John Hopkins University Press.

Rachlin, H. (1980). Economics and behavioural psychology. In J. E. R. Staddon (Ed.), *Limits to action*. New York: Academic Press.

Rachlin, H., & Green, L. (1972). Commitment, choice and self control. *Journal of the Experimental Analysis of Behavior*, *17*, 15–22.

Rachlin, H., Kagel, J. H., & Battalio, R. C. (1980). Substitutability in time allocation. *Psychological Review*, *87*, 355–374.

Robertson, H. M. (1933). *Aspects of the rise of economic individualism*. Cambridge, UK: Cambridge University Press.

Rogoff, B. (1990). *Apprenticeship in thinking*. New York: Oxford University Press.

Rogoff, B., & Wertsch, J. V. (1984). *Children's learning in the "zone of proximal development"*. San Francisco: Jossey-Bass.

Schelling, T. (1984). Self-command in practice, in policy, and in a theory of rational choice. *American Economic Review*, May, 1–11.

Schnieder, W. (1985). Developmental trends in the meta-memory behavior relationship: an integrative review. In D. L. Forrest-Pressley, G. E. Mackinnon, & T. G. Waller (Eds.), *Metacognition, cognition and human performance*. (Vol. 1). New York: Academic Press.

Schwartz, B. (1975). *Queuing and waiting: studies in the social organization of access and delay*. Chicago: University of Chicago Press.

Sharpe, C. (1981). *The economics of time*. Oxford: Martin Robertson.

Shefrin, H., & Thaler R. M. (1988). The behavioral life-cycle hypothesis. *Economic Inquiry, 66*, 609–43.

Shweder, R. A. (1982). Beyond self constructed knowledge: the study of culture and morality. *Merrill-Palmer Quarterly, 28*, 41–69.

Siegal, M. (1981). Children's perception of adult economic need. *Child Development, 52*, 379–392.

Signel, K. A. (1966). Cognitive complexity in person perception and nation perception: A developmental approach. *Journal of Personality, 34*, 517–537.

Simmons, P. J. (1974). *Choice and demand*. London: Macmillan.

Smiles, S. (1875). *Thrift*. London: Murray.

Sonuga-Barke, E. J. S. (1988). Misinterpreting Mischel. *Behavioral & Brain Sciences, 11*, 693–694.

Sonuga-Barke, E. J. S., Lea, S. E. G., & Webley, P. (1989). The development of adaptive choice in a self control paradigm *Journal of the Experimental Analysis of Behavior, 51*, 77–85.

Sonuga-Barke, E. J. S., Webley, P., & Lea, S. E. G. (1989). Children's choice; Sensitivity to reinforcer density. *Journal of the Experimental Analysis of Behavior, 51*, 185–197.

Stacey, B. G. (1982). Economic socialization in the pre-adult years. *British Journal of Social Psychology, 53*, 37–46.

Staddon, J. E. R. (1980). *Limits to action*. New York: Academic Press.

Strauss, A. (1952). The development and transformation of monetary meaning in the child. *American Sociological Review, 17*, 275–286.

Strauss, A. (1954). The development of conceptions of rules in children. *Child Development, 25*, 193–208.

Strotz, R. H. (1956). Myopia and inconsistencies in dynamic utility maximization. *Review of Economic Studies, 23*, 166–180.

Sutton, R. S. (1962). Behavior in the attainment of economic concepts. *Journal of Psychology, 5*, 37–46.

Tan, H. K., & Stacey, B. (1981). The understanding of socio-economic concepts in Malaysian Chinese school children. *Child Study Journal, 11*, 33–49.

Thaler, R. (1990). Anomalies: Saving, fungibility and mental accounts. *Journal of Economic Perspectives, 4*, 193–206.

Thaler, R., & Shefrin, H. M. (1981). An economic theory of self-control *Journal of Political Economy*, April, 392–406.

Thurow, L. (1969). The optimum lifetime distribution of consumption expenditures. *American Economic Review, 59*, 334–340.

Trevarthen, C. (1988). Universal co-operative motives: How infants begin to know the language and culture of their parents. In G. Jahoda & I. M. Lewis (Eds.), *Acquiring culture: Cross cultural studies in child development*. London: Croom Helm.

Turiel, E., Killen, M., & Helwig, C. (1987). Morality: its structure, function, and vagaries. In J. Kagan & S. Lamb (Eds.), *Morality in young children*. Chicago: University of Chicago Press.

Tysoe, M. (1983). Children and Money. *New Society, 66*, 433–444.

Valsiner, J. (1987). *Culture and the development of children's action: A cultural historical theory of developmental psychology*. New York: Wiley.

Valsiner, J. (1988). Ontogeny of co-construction of culture within socially organized environmental settings. In J. Valsiner (Ed.). *Child development within culturally structured environments (Vol. 2)*. Norwood, NJ: Ablex.

Valsiner, J., & Benigni, L. (1986). Naturalistic research and ecological thinking in the study of child development. *Development Review, 6*, 203–223.

Vidal, F. (1987). Jean Piaget and the liberal protestant tradition. In M. Ash and W. Woodward (Eds.), *Psychology in 20th century thought and society*. Cambridge, UK: Cambridge University Press.

Vosniadou, S., & Brewer, W. F. (1987). Theories of knowledge restructuring in development. *Review of Educational Research, 57*, 51–67.

Vygotsky, L. S. (1987). Thinking and speech. In R. W. Rieber & A. S. Carton (Eds.), *The collected works of L. S. Vygotsky*. (N. Minick trans.). New York: Plenum Press.

Ward, S., Wackman, D. B., & Wartella, E. (1977). *How children learn to buy*. London: Sage.

Weber, M. (1976). *The protestant ethic and the spirit of capitalism*. (Originally published 1904). London: Allen & Unwin.

Weber, W. (1975). Interest rates, inflation and consumer expenditures. *American Economic Review, 65*, 843–858.

Webley, P., & Webley, E. (1990). The playground economy. In S. E. G. Lea, P. Webley, & B. Young (Eds.), *Applied economic psychology in the 1990's*. Exeter: Washington Singer Press.

Weinraub, M., Brooks, J., & Lamb, M. (1977). The social network: a reconsideration of the concept of attachment. *Human Development, 20*, 31–47.

Wellman, H. M. (1977). Preschoolers' understanding of memory relevant variables. *Child Development, 48*, 13–21.

Wellman, H. M. (1985). The child's theory of mind: The development of conceptions of cognition. In S. R.Yussen (Ed.), *The growth of reflection in children*. Orlando, FL: Academic Press.

Wertsch, J. V., & Youniss, J. (1987). Contextualizing the investigator: the case of developmental psychology. *Human Development, 30*, 18–31.

West, L. H. T., & Pine, A. L. (1985). *Cognitive structure and conceptual change*. New York: Academic Press.

Author Index

Abercrombie, N., 65, 129
Ainslie, G., 119
Antonides, G., 117

Bandura, A., 117
Bentham, J., 130
Berti, A.E., 15, 93, 121, 126, 131, 132, 133, 135
Boehm-Bewark, E. von, 18
Bombi, A.S., 121
Boulding, K., 130
Brim, O., 105
Bronfenbrenner, U., 107, 108, 109, 110, 111

Carrol, C., 119
Case, R., 96
Clower, R.W., 11
Connell, R.W., 94
Cordes, J.J., 120
Courant, P., 119
Cowling, K., 67

Danziger, K., 92
DeBeni, R., 93
Dickins, D., 13

Ferenczi, S., 12
Ferguson, C.E., 13
Fisher, I., 18
Freidman, M., 11, 65
Freud, S., 12, 116
Furnham, A., 13
Furth, H., 92

Galin, M., 111
Galper, H., 120
Goldstein, B., 15
Gramlich, E., 119

Hausman, J., 117
Hill, S., 65, 129
Hussein, G., 72

Jahoda, G., 3, 4, 92, 101, 102
Jenks, C., 127
Johnson, M.B., 11

Katona, G., 10, 11, 68
Kessen, W., 65
Keynes, J.M., 10, 11, 66, 114
Kirby, S.N., 120
Kotlitoff, L., 119

Kourilsky, M., 122
Kurz, M., 117

La Fontaine, J. de., 66
Laitner, J., 119
Lancaster, K.J., 68
Lea, S.E.G., 65, 66
Leiser, D., 93, 115

Maital, S., 15, 18, 119, 126, 127, 133
Maital, S.L., 15, 126, 127, 133
Marshall, A., 106
McCloskey, D.N., 65
McGuiness, T., 67
Mill, J.S., 130
Mischel, W., 14, 15, 116, 117

Nelson, K., 3, 4, 93
Newson, E., 15
Newson, J., 15
Ng, S.H., 101

Oldham, J., 15

Piaget, J., 92, 96, 97, 103, 127, 128

Rogoff, B., 131, 135

Schelling, T., 118
Shefrin, H., 119
Signal, K.A., 5
Smiles, S., 66
Sonuga-Barke, E.J.S., 12, 91, 102, 103,
    104, 106, 107, 113, 114, 115, 116, 117,
    118, 121, 122, 123
Spencer, H., 130
Spiegelman, R.G., 117
Strauss, A., 92
Summers, L.H., 119

Tarpy, R., 65
Thaler, R.M., 119
Thomas, P., 13
Turner, T., 65, 129
Tysoe, M., 13

Valsiner, J., 115

Ward, S., 13, 15
Weber, M., 130
Webley, P., 65, 91, 102, 103, 104, 106,
    107, 113, 114, 115, 116, 117, 118, 121,
    122, 123
West, R.W., 117
Woerdenbagch, A., 3

Subject Index

Adult economy, 4, 5
Arithmetical ability,
   and saving, 98

Bank,
   accounts, 48, 85
   child's understanding of, 3, 4,
   100–103
   piggy, 44, 49, 61–62
Banking, 53, 56–57, 61, 73, 79–81
Behaviour modification, 83
Building societies, 68

Child-centred approach to study, 5, 6,
12, 85–88, 137
Children's saving, studies of, 9
Cognitive developmentalism,
   and cognitive psychology, 93, 104,
   126–127
   and economic socialisation, 2, 4, 7,
   100
   and naive realism, 2
   and neo-Piagetian theory, 1, 86,
   91–93, 108, 126–133
Cognition and moral obligation, 96

Cognitive development, 3
Cognitive psychology, 93, 104, 126–127
Collecting and saving, 72
Consumption and saving, 45
Contextualism, 134–135
Cross-cultural studies, 106, 114–116,
131–133
Cultural influences on development,
86, 131–133

Delay of gratification, 11–14, 18,
116–118
Developmental economic psychology, 1
Developmental psychology, western,
125

Ecological approaches, 108–114
Economic,
   cultural significance of, 1, 4, 5, 6
   definitions of, 5, 6
   education, 104, 121–122, 133–134
   formal aspects of, 7
   functional aspects of, 7
   historical significance of, 5, 7
   man, 65–66, 106–107, 129–130

practical significance of, 1, 4, 6, 7, 8,
15, 128–130
  ideals, 1, 5, 9, 15, 65–66
    western, 7
  socialisation, 2, 4, 7, 9, 100
Economics, 65
  Capitalist, 133–134
  Islamic, 133–134
  Marxist, 133–134
  socio-biology, 130
Economic problem solver, the child as,
6, 9, 105, 128–130

Family, the, as a context for economic
development, 60

Hiding,
  and saving, 38
History,
  and developmental psychology, 2

Impulsiveness,
  children's understanding of, 25
  and saving, 18, 20
Income constraint, 6, 13, 17, 51, 59, 87,
113
Interest,
  child's understanding of, 3
  as rewards, 70–71
  and saving, 53, 57–58, 61–62, 67–68,
  70, 101

Marketeers' understanding of economic
acts, 63
Marketing strategies, 66–73
Metaknowledge, 18, 19, 27
Money,
  children's understanding of, 4

Neo-Piagetian theory, 1, 86, 91–93,
108, 126–133

Parents,
  and behaviour modification, 83
  role in economic developments, 5,
  49–51
  and saving, 58–59, 75–84

understanding of economics, 63,
73–84
Permanent income hypothesis, 11
Play economies, the status of, 49–50,
59–62, 95–99
Pocket money, 48–49, 59, 73–74,
76–77, 100–102
Profit, child's understanding of, 3
Protestant work ethic, 12, 129–130

Rationality, 66
  different approaches to, 85–89
Resource allocation,
  and income constraint, 6, 87, 113
  problems of, 6, 110–111
  and time constraint, 7, 113
  and utility maximisation, 7, 8, 66, 87

Siblings, 49
Social representations of economic
actions, 5, 63–84
  and history, 65–66
  marketeers', 63
  parents', 63, 73–84
Socio-biology, 130
Socio-developmentalism, 2, 5, 93–95,
100, 107–108, 125–137
  and child-centred approach to study,
  5, 6, 12, 85–88, 137
  and contextualism, 134–135
  and saving, 12, 15, 59
  and socio-functionalism, 2, 134–135
Socio-functionalism, 2, 134–135
Stage theories,
  of cognitive development, 3
  of economic development, 4
Saving, 12, 15, 59
  accounts, 13
  and arithmetical ability, 98
  and banking, 53, 56–57, 61, 73,
  79–81
  children's understanding of, 4, 96,
  100–102, 105
  and collecting, 72
  and commitment, 20
  as consumer good, 68
  and consumption, 45

contractual and discretionary, 10, 13, 77–81
definitions of, 10, 118–119
and delay of gratification, 11–14, 18, 116–118
demographic variations in, 12, 60
development of functional, 17, 23–32, 52–61, 78, 85, 99–100
everyday significance of, 44
and family, 60
functional and nonfunctional, 11, 12, 13, 15, 43, 69, 71, 132–133
habit, 70, 72–73, 83, 85, 113, 132
and hiding, 38
as hobby, 71
and impulsiveness, 18, 20
and income constraints, 13, 17, 43, 51, 59
institutionalised, 44, 66–73
and interest, 53, 57–58, 61–62, 67–68, 70, 105
as loss of money, 26, 44, 52
and metaknowledge, 18, 19, 27
motives, for, 10
parental influence on, 75–84
plans, 18
and protestant work ethic, 12, 129–130
as remedy for economic madness, 81–83
the rhetoric of, 64, 66
and self control, 10, 20
as socially acceptable goal, 11, 60–61, 69, 72, 74, 79, 87
and spending, 81–83, 98
strategic aspects of, 14, 18, 19, 25, 33, 41, 45, 54–60
and subjective interest rate, 116–118
and temptation, 14, 18, 20, 26, 27, 31, 32, 39–40, 45, 51, 79, 85, 103
and theft, 54, 58, 81, 85, 101–102
theories of adult, 11, 12, 119–121
and thrift, 13, 64, 66, 69, 103, 105, 130
and time preference, 116–118
voluntary and involuntary, 10
Self control, 10, 20
SES as factor in development, 12, 60, 110–111
Spending,
    and saving, 81–83, 98
Stock market crash, 107
Subjective interest rate, 116–118

Temptation, 14, 18, 20, 26, 27, 31, 32, 39–40, 45, 51, 79, 85, 103
Theft, 54, 58, 81, 85, 101–102
Thrift, 13, 64, 66, 69, 103, 105, 130
Time constraint, 7, 113
Time preference, 116–118

Utility maximisation, 7, 8, 66

Value,
    economic ideas of, 27, 32, 33, 34–41, 132–133
    social ideas of, 27, 32, 34–41, 132–133

Other Titles in the Series
Essays in Developmental Psychology
Series Editors: Peter Bryant, George Butterworth, Harry McGurk

ANALOGICAL REASONING IN CHILDREN

USHA GOSWAMI
(University of Cambridge)

Analogical reasoning is a fundamental cognitive skill, involved in classification, learning, problem-solving and creative thinking, and should be a basic building block of cognitive development. However, for a long time researchers have believed that children are incapable of reasoning by analogy. This book argues that this is far from the case, and that analogical reasoning may be available very early in development. Recent research has shown that even 3-year-olds can solve analogies, and that infants can reason about relational similarity, which is the hallmark of analogy.

The book traces the roots of the popular misconceptions about children's analogical abilities and argues that when children fail to use analogies, it is because they do not understand the relations underlying the analogy rather than because they are incapable of analogical reasoning. The author argues that young children spontaneously use analogies in learning, and that their analogies can sometimes lead them into misconceptions. In the "real worlds" of their classrooms, children use analogies when learning basic skills like reading, and even babies seem to use analogies to learn about the world around them.

Contents: Reasoning by Analogy. Structural Theories of Analogical Development. Testing the Claims of Structural Theory. Information-Processing Accounts of Classical Analogical Reasoning. Problem Analogies and Analogical Development. Analogies in Babies and Toddlers. Analogies in the Real World of the Classroom.

ISBN 0-86377-226-9 1992 144pp. $28.50 £14.95 hbk

Please send USA & Canadian orders to: Lawrence Erlbaum Associates Inc., 365 Broadway, Hillsdale, New Jersey, NJ07642, USA. For UK & Rest of World, please send orders to: Lawrence Erlbaum Associates Ltd., Mail Order Department, 27 Church Road, Hove, East Sussex, BN3 2FA, England. Note, prices shown here are correct at time of going to press, but may change. Prices outside Europe may differ from those shown.

Other Titles in the Series
Essays in Developmental Psychology
Series Editors: Peter Bryant, George Butterworth, Harry McGurk

THE DEVELOPMENT OF YOUNG CHILDREN'S SOCIAL-COGNITIVE SKILLS

MICHAEL A. FORRESTER
(University of Kent)

Understanding how young children begin to make sense out of the social world has become a major concern within developmental psychology. Over the last 25 years research in this area has raised a number of questions which mirror the confluence of interests from cognitive-developmental and social-developmental psychology. The aims of this book are to critically consider the major themes and findings within this growing social-cognitive developmental research, and to present a new theoretical framework for investigating children's social cognitive skills. Beyond being the first major review of the literature in this area, this synopsis articulates why contemporary theoretical ideas (e.g. information processing, Piagetian and social interactionist) are unlikely ever to provide the conceptual basis for understanding children's participative skills.

Building upon ideas both within and beyond mainstream developmental psychology, the "eco-structural" approach advocated seeks to draw together the advantages of the ecological approach in perceptual psychology with the considerable insights of the conversational analysts, child language researchers and Goffman's analysis of social interaction. This convergence is centred around the dynamic and participatory realities of engaging in conversational contexts, the locus for acquiring social cognitive skills.

The framework provides the building blocks for models of developmental social cognition which can accommodate dynamic aspects of children's conversational skills. This book then is a review of an important area of developmental psychology, a new perspective on how we can study children's participatory social-cognitive skills and a summary of supporting research for the framework advocated.

ISBN 0-86377-232-3 1992 176pp. $25.50 £14.95 hbk.

Please send USA & Canadian orders to: Lawrence Erlbaum Associates Inc., 365 Broadway, Hillsdale, New Jersey, NJ07642, USA. For UK & Rest of World, please send orders to: Lawrence Erlbaum Associates Ltd., Mail Order Department, 27 Church Road, Hove, East Sussex, BN3 2FA, England. Note, prices shown here are correct at time of going to press, but may change. Prices outside Europe may differ from those shown.